MEMORIES OF A FORWARD AIR CONTROLLER

BY
TOM PETITMERMET

MEMORIES OF A FORWARD AIR CONTROLLER

Copyright © 2019 Tom Petitmermet

All rights reserved. No part of this book may be reproduced or utilized in any form or by any means, electronic or mechanical, including photocopying and recording, or by any information storage and retrieval system, without permission in writing from the publisher.

First Edition

Because of the dynamic nature of the internet, any web address or links contained in this book may have changed since publication and may no longer be valid.

The views expressed in this work are soley those of the author and do not necessarily reflect the views of the publisher, and the publisher hereby disclaims any responsibility for them.

Published by Tactical 16, LLC
Colorado Springs, CO

ISBN: 978-1-943226-35-1 (paperback)

Contents

Chapter 1
A Perfect Plan — 1

Chapter 2
Pipeline to the War — 5

Chapter 3
Preparation for War — 11

Chapter 4
Finally Arrived at the War — 21

Chapter 5
Quan Loi, The Garden Spot in Southeast Asia — 37

Chapter 6
Flying Combat Missions in Cambodia — 47

Chapter 7
Conducting an Air Strike — 55

Chapter 8
Other Missions I Flew in Cambodia and Vietnam — 79

Chapter 9
Other Very Unique Events During My War — 93

Chapter 10
After Thoughts About the War — 125

Chapter 11
Honoring My Fallen Brothers in Arms — 129

Chapter 1
A PERFECT PLAN

During the Vietnam era (1965-1975) one of the choices facing most young males in the United States was what to do after graduation from high school: go to college or get drafted into the military to fight in a very unpopular war. I graduated from Central Catholic High School in Portland, Oregon in June 1965 and really had very little choice about my options. I applied to the University of Portland, following in the footsteps of my brother Jim who was four years ahead of me. Jim was in the Air Force Reserve Officer Training Corps (ROTC) with the expressed intent of not getting drafted into the Army and going to Vietnam. Since that looked like a very good plan, I also joined the Air Force ROTC program with the same intention of not getting drafted into the Army or going to Vietnam. I had a college deferment (2-S) from the draft as long as I was enrolled in college. A good number of my friends who decided that they needed a break from school and dropped out were immediately drafted into the Army.

This was a very turbulent time in the U.S. There were many anti-war protests around the country, including at my very conservative college. As a matter of fact, in the early spring of 1968 our ROTC building was torched by some student Vietnam War protestors. The ROTC Detachment lost some papers, books, and equipment but still had a functional building for training. We would occasionally get taunts from other students when we wore our Air Force ROTC uniforms on campus. It was a very tough time to be a student in the late sixties.

I was pretty loose and carefree during my first three semesters in college. I put academics on the back burner and really had my golf game in order. I managed to play golf at least two times a week no matter my class schedule. The problem was that my grade point average (GPA) was a very paltry 2.2. The sergeant in charge of the cadets at the ROTC program brought me into his office and explained that without a GPA of at least 2.5 I would not be allowed to continue in the ROTC program my junior year. So, I needed to get my butt in gear and get my grades up in the second semester of my sophomore year. The sergeant came up with a plan for me to do just that. It would not be easy, but it could be done. He walked me through the classes I needed to take—twenty-four credit hours of very tough academic course work. He also required me to check in with him three times a week and give him an update on how the classes were going. It was a very tough course load but through a lot of hard work and no golf that semester I achieved a 3.80 average (even with the useless Philosophy class) on my class work and brought my grades up to a respectable, for me, 2.85. The study habits and discipline that the sergeant taught me really paid off for the rest of my days in college.

The ROTC curriculum was broken down into two phases. The first phase during my freshman and sophomore years was called the General Military Course; the second phase during junior and senior years was called the Professional Officer Course. Specific topics included Foundations of the Air Force, The Evolution of Aerospace Studies, Leadership Studies, National Security Studies, and Preparation for Active Duty. In addition to the classroom work, we had a formal workout program to get us ready for the annual Air Force Fitness Test. The test was nothing too strenuous. The physical training (PT) was just part of the program to become an Air Force officer.

During the summer after my junior year I was off to ROTC summer camp at Fairchild Air Force Base in Spokane, Washington. The two-week camp was our basic training, but much less intense than the real Air Force basic training. We learned how to march, to work together as a team and to study, in much more detail, the finer points of the Air Force. We were exposed to many of the functions of the Air Force, but I still had no idea of what I really wanted to do once I was commissioned. All of the different jobs I was exposed to were acceptable to me as they weren't in the Army and had no expectation of sending me to Vietnam. My plan to avoid the draft, the Army, and Vietnam was paying off. I could see myself in a very cushy stateside Air Force assignment.

So as the years moved on, the U.S. Selective Service program came up with a more "equitable" draft by instituting the lottery system. Each young male eighteen years or older was assigned a draft number based on their birth date. The Selective Service would then decide how many individuals they needed for a specific calendar year and would draft anyone eligible with a certain draft number below the establish cutoff date. The lottery numbers ranged from one to 366. The lower the number, the more likely you would get drafted. So here I was merrily moving along in my college career and also in my Air Force ROTC career.

In my junior year of college, the ROTC protocol was to take the military entrance physical and the comprehensive Air Force Officer's Qualification

Test (AFOQT) to determine just where we may end up in the Air Force. My test scores were all in the nineties for pilot and or navigator aptitude, and I was fully medically qualified to be a pilot. My plan was still good: I would be joining the Air Force upon graduation in May 1969 to avoid the draft and be free from Vietnam duty.

I guess another omen of things to come was my draft lottery number for the 1969 lottery: 299. Since I had already committed to at least four years in the Air Force, the high lottery number that was selected for my birthday was a moot point. The Selective Service that year only drafted up to number 208. I would have dodged the bullet with that number, but I was on my way to the Air Force… how bad could that be? I was notified in the middle of my senior year that, based on my AFOQT scores and being medically qualified for pilot training, I would be assigned to a pilot training class upon graduation in May 1969. As it turned out, my strategy to avoid the Army and Vietnam did not work out as planned.

Chapter 2
PIPELINE TO THE WAR

The story of my assignment as a Forward Air Controller (FAC) really began to take a focused shape during my time in Undergraduate Pilot Training (UPT) in Lubbock, Texas. UPT was the primary training program for Air Force pilots, and during the 1969-1970 time frame the UPT training program lasted for a very long fifty-three weeks.

I did have some very minimal flying time (thirty-six hours) when I arrived at Reese Air Force Base on May 15, 1969, to start UPT. During my senior year in Air Force Reserve Officer Training Corps (ROTC) at the University of Portland I participated in and completed my initial Air Force flying training in the Flight Instruction Program or (FIP). This program was designed to ensure future Air Force pilot training candidates had the aptitude to complete the formal UPT program. It was also much cheaper to screen future pilots in a civilian flying environment before sending them to the formal, and expensive, UPT classes. So here I was with my first set of Air Force wings. The problem was the ROTC FIP wings looked just like the wings that stewardesses gave to little kids on their first commercial flight. I was reluctant to wear them in public.

During the FIP program we trained in a Cessna C-150 aircraft. It was a two-seat, single-engine general aviation, high-wing aircraft that was perfect for learning the basics of flying. The C-150 was twenty-three feet long, had a thirty-three-foot wingspan, a Continental 0-200, 100-horsepower engine with a maximum speed of 125 miles per hour, and a maximum fully loaded weight of around 1,600 pounds. We flew our training flights out of Portland International Airport among the mix of many commercial airline and general aviation flights.

The flying program involved many hours of ground school, dual flight instruction time, solo traffic patterns, solo aerobatic flights, and a solo cross-country flight. I flew my first solo flight on October 9, 1968, and finished the FIP program with fifteen hours of solo flight out of a total of thirty-six hours of flight time. My solo cross-country check ride flight was to Eugene, Oregon, a little more than one hundred miles south of Portland. Fortunately, Interstate 5 follows the flight path almost perfectly to and from Portland, so I didn't get lost on my solo cross-country flight.

After completing the FIP, I graduated from the University of Portland and the ROTC program on May 10, 1969, as a Distinguished AFROTC Graduate–thanks to the superb study program the ROTC sergeant put in place for me. I arrived Reese Air Force Base in Lubbock, Texas for UPT on May 15, 1969.

For a good old boy from green and mountainous Oregon, Lubbock was quite a shock. This part of Texas is as flat as a pancake, very dusty with lots of prevailing winds, and hotter than it ever was in Oregon. But this is where I started my flying career. As I got to know the other Second Lieutenants in my class, there were one hundred of us, I realized that ninety-eight percent of the class were recent graduates from Officer Training School (OTS) who had joined the Air Force to avoid the draft, the Army, and Vietnam. That sounded a lot like my plan to avoid Vietnam. A lot of the folks I talked to did not want to be at UPT but had agreed to the training since that was their only way into the Air Force and not the Army. This reluctance became quite apparent during the opening meeting with the future pilots. As were called to attention when the Flying Wing Commander, Colonel Clyde Morganti, entered the room to address the class, one of the students "fainted." This individual was immediately dropped from the UPT class and sent to a non-flying job somewhere in the Air Force. What a way to start your first day of active duty service…I believe this was a planned event on the part of the person that fainted.

So, there I was ready to become the world's greatest pilot. But first there were a number of introductory ground school classes that I had to take before I even stepped foot on the flight line.

My first introduction to Air Force flying was in the Cessna T-41 Mescalero. The T-41 was the Air Force version of a civilian general aviation aircraft also known as the C-172. The T-41 was a high-wing aircraft, twenty-seven feet long, with a wingspan of thirty-six feet, a maximum weight of 2,450 pounds, and a maximum speed of 144 miles per hour with a 160-horsepower engine. My training class was bussed to Lubbock Municipal Airport for all of our T-41 flying. Most of the instructors were civilian pilots, and I was impressed by my west Texas cowboy instructor who wore the most beat up cowboy boots I had even seen. As T-41 pilots, we were required to wear low-quarter shoes so we could have a better feel for the airplane rudder pedals. The low-quarter shoes were a dead giveaway to everyone that we were in our initial stages of pilot training. Almost to a man, as soon as the flying day was over and we returned to Reese Air Force Base, we all changed into our regular issued flying boots…they made us look cool.

My first flight in the T-41 was on June 5, 1970, and my last flight was on July 2, 1970. Our flight instruction included traffic pattern flights, aerobatic flights, and stalls and falls; I completed three hours of solo flight time in the T-41. The OTS candidates in my class got a few more introductory flight hours as they had not gone through the FIP program like I did in ROTC.

Once we were finished and passed the T-41 phase of flying, it was on to the mighty Cessna T-37 jet trainer. The T-37 was a side-by-side seating aircraft that was twenty-nine feet long with a thirty-three-foot wingspan and a maximum weight of 6,569 pounds. The T-37 was powered by two J-69 turbojet engines that produced 1,025 pounds of thrust each. The T-37 had a maximum speed of 369 knots and a service ceiling of 35,000 feet. For the first time I would be flying an aircraft that used knots per hour rather than miles per hour. Knots are typically used in maritime and aviation, and one knot per hour is equivalent to 1.15 miles per hour.

But not so fast! Before we could start flying the T-37 we had many hours of ground school to get us ready for the next step in our flying career. The many ground school topics included Aviation Physiology, T-37 System Operations, Principles of Flight, Aural Code (Morse Code), Flight Instruments, Instruments and Radio Aids, Navigation, Flight Planning, Flying Safety, and Weather.

One other important training topic was the use of an ejection seat and survival equipment, as well as how to do a successful parachute landing fall. After many jumps from a short tower in the hard Texas ground, we had the ultimate training: parasailing in the Texas countryside. We were strapped into a parachute harness and hooked to the back of a pickup truck by a 200-foot rope. The truck accelerated and we would get airborne in our parachute. The main goal was to fall the last one hundred feet or so for an actual parachute landing. The biggest challenge was to avoid all of the cactus plants that were in our landing zone. I successfully completed this portion of the training and was more than ready to fly the T-37. Some of the students in our class were not so lucky, and two pilot candidates broke their legs during this training and were reassigned until they could heal properly.

Before I had my first flight in a jet aircraft, I had to complete numerous hours in the Link Flight Simulator. The simulator was an excellent tool to learn all the various switches and controls in the T-37. We went through engine start, taxi, take off, in-flight maneuvers, and landings. Included in every single simulator flight was a review of various inflight emergencies that could arise during actual flight.

After I was deemed proficient enough to fly a jet aircraft I was paired with an Air Force Flight instructor to begin my training in earnest. My first flight on August 11, 1969, was very exhilarating and I knew right then that I wanted to be an Air Force pilot. When my instructor asked if there was any maneuver that I wanted to try, I immediately told him I wanted to see a spin. What a ride. A spin is a maneuver where you lose complete control of the aircraft and then use very specific flight control movements to get out of the spin. A spin is something that you practice but never want to get into while flying. The training included practice take offs and landings, aerobatic maneuvers, instrument flying, and initial instruction in formation flying. I accumulated fifteen hours of solo time in the T-37.

One of the areas that I really excelled at was instrument flying. I knew I was doing fairly well in this phase of training as I had a different instructor for nearly every single instrument flight. One instructor really stood out in this instrument phase of training. He would always tell me "Cross check, cross check, cross check," which meant to watch my attitude indicator, vertical velocity indicator, and turn needle. Because of his training, I actually did quite well in the instrument phase of the T-37 and earned the "Skunderdud" award with one of the highest instrument check ride scores in my class.

We had many hours to talk about the Air Force and flying, and this instructor asked me what kind of airplane I wanted to fly after I got my wings. I told him I would love to fly a fighter aircraft. He said that would be a good choice but very few fighter aircraft had been coming down in the assignment process. He recommended that, if available, I should consider a Forward Air Controller (FAC) assignment if no fighters were available in my assignment block. He said that in many cases the FACs would get a follow-on assignment to a fighter aircraft. At the time I didn't know what a FAC assignment meant. This recommendation would come true for my first flying assignment and played a very huge role in a mission I would fly two years later in Southeast Asia.

Following completion of the T-37 phase of training it was on to the really impressive training aircraft, the T-38. The T-38 Talon was a Northrup-built jet trainer, a two-seat supersonic aircraft cable of speeds up to Mach 1.3. At forty-six feet long, it had a twenty-five-foot wingspan and a maximum weight of 11,850 pounds. It was powered by two J-85 jet engines capable of generating nearly 2,900 pounds of thrust in afterburner.

As in the T-37, before flight I spent many hours in the T-38 simulator working on switchology, controls, and emergency procedures. The ground school for the T-38 covered aviation physiology, systems operations, applied aerodynamics, and flight planning. Similar to the T-37, flight training in the T-38 included takeoff and landing practice, aerobatic flight maneuvers, and an enhanced formation flying portion. We started out in two-ship formation flights and eventually worked our way up to four-ship formation flying. This formation flying was both dual and solo sorties.

My first T-38 flight was on January 15, 1970, and I had a little more than thirty-one hours of solo time in the T-38. One very exciting series of flights was my dual cross-country flight to Hamilton Air Force Base near San Francisco, California. I flew with an instructor pilot and we made two stops along the way at Luke Air Force Base near Phoenix and North Island Naval Air Station in San Diego. On our last leg into Hamilton we filed for a low-level flight along the coast of California. We flew at 3,000 feet about one mile off the shore and saw the incredible splendor of the California coast. Landing near San Francisco was a real thrill as we flew very near the Golden Gate Bridge on our approach and landing at Hamilton.

As graduation time approached, we focused on many different aspects of flying including cross country flights, both dual and solo, and many hours of formation flying. By the time the flying program was finished I had 211 hours of Air Force flying time. One thing that I was a little bit disappointed in was my first time flying at supersonic speeds. The only cue that I had was the airspeed indicator which showed we passed the sound barrier and were flying at 1.1 Mach, or 1.1 times the speed of sound.

Now came the interesting part of the UPT experience: our aircraft assignments. As I mentioned earlier, my UPT Class 70-07 started with one hundred students. By the time the fifty-three weeks were up we were down to just fifty-one students that would graduate. The class was reduced in size primarily due to a thing called Self-Initiated Elimination (SIE) whereby a student could voluntarily drop from the program. There were many reasons for the large number of SIE's in our class including not wanting to be a pilot, the fear of flying, medical reasons, and lack of aptitude for flying. So on aircraft assignment day, all fifty-one of us were called into a classroom and on the black board at the front of the room was a list of fifty-one aircraft. One by one, from the first in the class to the last in class. we walked up to the front of the room and wrote our name next to the aircraft we selected.

As predicted by my instrument instructor, there was only one fighter aircraft available to our class. Number two in the class selected the F-4 Phantom. By the time I selected my aircraft, there were not too many options available that I wanted. There were a bunch of bombers, tanker aircraft, and cargo aircraft available. I did not want to fly a "heavy" aircraft. I remembered again what my instrument instructor told me about a Forward Air Controller (FAC) assignment. Take a FAC assignment and get a fighter on your next assignment. So, I selected a FAC assignment, a 0-2A. My plan to avoid Vietnam was officially dead because now I had to report there on December 31, 1970.

Chapter 3
PREPARATION FOR WAR

I was awarded my pilot wings on May 27, 1970, along with a detailed set of orders outlining the many additional training courses I needed to take before reporting to Vietnam. Those courses included Basic Survival Training at Fairchild Air Force Base, Washington, Fighter Lead-In Training at Cannon Air Force Base, New Mexico, Water Survival Training at Homestead Air Force Base, Florida, Cessna 0-2 Skymaster training at Hurlburt Field, Florida, and finally Jungle Survival Training at Clark Air Force Base in the Philippines.

Since I grew up in the northwest, I felt survival school in Washington state would fit my experience level perfectly. Little did I know that the survival portion of the school would be the easy part of the program. The real name of the program was Survival, Evasion, Resistance and Escape (SERE) School. One of the main functions of the survival course was to learn how to handle the psychological and physical stress of survival. Those of us that were on our way to the war in Southeast Asia were caught right in the middle of some very intense training scenarios. The thought was that those of us in an aircraft who had a very high probability of getting shot down were the prime candidates for this intense SERE training. There was a lot of classroom course work on proper techniques for survival, evasion, resistance, and escape.

Those classroom sessions were the easy part. The field exercises that followed each one of those principles were the difficult part of the training. We were taught the basics of post-ejection or bailout procedures and how to handle parachute landings. We also had material presented to us on survival medicine, shelter construction, gathering and cooking food, land navigation methods, evasion and camouflage, signaling, and aircraft vectoring.

During a four-day period we were exposed to what it would be like if were held as a prisoner of war (POW), complete with intense interrogation, confinement in a prison-like environment, and generally tough treatment of the students. The concept of this training was how to survive and resist the enemy in the event of being captured.

I think it is important to list the six basic tenets of the Military Code of Conduct that we were required to memorize in case we were captured by the enemy:

1. I am an American, fighting in the forces which guard my country and our way of life. I am prepared to give my life in their defense.
2. I will never surrender of my own free will. If in command, I will never surrender the members of my command while they still have the means to resist.
3. If I am captured, I will continue to resist by all means available. I will make every effort to escape and to aid others to escape. I will accept neither parole nor special favors from the enemy.
4. If I become a prisoner of war, I will keep faith with my fellow prisoners. I will give no information nor take part in any action which might be harmful to my comrades. If I am senior, I will take command. If not, I will obey the lawful orders of those appointed over me and will back them up in every way.
5. When questioned, should I become a prisoner of war, I am required to give name, rank, service number, and date of birth. I will evade answering further questions to the utmost of my ability; I will make no oral or written statements disloyal to my country and its allies or harmful to their cause.
6. I will never forget that I am an American, fighting for freedom, responsible for my actions, and dedicated to the principles which made my country free. I will trust in my God and in the United States of America.

I knew I wouldn't die in the training as they needed pilots for the war, but it was fairly realistic, and I learned that I was somewhat claustrophobic when I was stuffed into a very small three-by-five-foot box for nearly six hours. I was just counting the hours as I knew I would be released the next day because we still had to go out to the field for the survival portion of the training. Nevertheless, it seemed realistic to me.

The actual survival portion of the training was a piece of cake for me as I had done a lot of camping and fishing in the Northwest and was familiar with many of the things that I was taught through my Boy Scout training. We "marched" for a few miles through the woods in teams of six. We had to make our own shelter, fix our own food, and learn from our instructor certain survival techniques that would keep us alive if we were shot down. I taught my team the important task of catching fish in one of the streams near our chosen campsite. We had caught so many rainbow trout that we shared them with the instructors. The instructors did provide us with one live rabbit that we had to kill and prepare for one of our meals. After we found some wild onions, we had quit a meal for our small group.

Next on the agenda was how to escape and evade capture from the enemy. We were taught concealment techniques and then given a map with instructions to make it to the check point in less than twelve hours. There were instructors all along the way trying to find us as we progressed to the designated pick-up point. It was kind of humorous as they knew the exact route we had to take and easily found each one of us as we made our way to the safe pick-up point. Once we all made it back to the pick-up point we were loaded on a bus and returned back to the base for a huge meal at the chow hall.

As the formal SERE portion of the class came to an end one of our instructors called out about thirty names, mine included, to stay behind for an important announcement. The head instructor announced that each one of us that were called out had the greatest likelihood of being shot down and taken prisoner during our assignment to Southeast Asia and told we were ordered to stay at the survival school an extra five days to learn a special code-writing technique in case we were taken prisoner. It was a very straight-forward class on how to imbed messages in letters that we would write home during our captivity. It took a lot of practice, and after the five days we all passed and told good luck with this program if we ever needed it.

My next stop in the long list of training courses was the Fighter Lead-In Training at Cannon Air Force Base in New Mexico. The Army and Air Force had established a policy that any bomb dropped near U.S. Army troops in Southeast Asia had to be controlled by a Forward Air Controller that was a qualified fighter pilot. There had been too many cases where bombs had been dropped on friendly forces during the fog of war. The Fighter Lead In program was designed to make us instant fighter pilots. Only about twenty-five percent of the FACs heading to Southeast Asia were selected to the Fighter Lead In program and were designated "A" FACS. The remaining FACs that didn't attend Fighter Lead in were designated "B" FACS and could only control missions in support of non-U.S. ground forces.

We were trained as fighter pilots in a very old post-WWII aircraft that was a converted AF trainer and designated the AT-33 Shooting Star. The AT-33 was thirty-seven feet long, had a wingspan of thirty-seven feet, and had a single J-33 turbojet engine that produced approximately 2,600 pounds of thrust. It had a maximum speed of 524 knots and a service ceiling of 48,000 feet. Since we were being trained to be fighter pilots, the AT-33 was equipped with two hard point mounts under the wings capable of carrying bombs or rockets. The AT-33 also had two Browning, M-3 12.7 mm, machine guns mounted in the nose of the aircraft.

Our training curriculum was fairly straight forward. We needed to learn how to fly the airplane first and then we had multiple flights to the gunnery range to perfect our bombing and strafing techniques. One of the biggest challenges flying the AT-33 was taxiing the aircraft as it had no powered nose-wheel steering. Pilots steered the airplane on the ground using differential braking. It required finesse to get to and from the takeoff, landing, and taxi back to the ramp without cocking the nose wheel. Many students cocked the nose wheel on many flights including their final check ride. Fortunately, I never once cocked the nose wheel at Cannon Air Force Base, though I did in a future assignment in the T-33 a few years later in my flying career. My first flight in the AT-33 was on July 13, 1970, my first solo was on July 27, 1970, and I had a total of 33.2 hours in the aircraft. I was designated a qualified fighter pilot on September 23, 1970.

A funny story happened while I was at Cannon Air Force Base. The wing Commander was retiring and many of his Air Force friends from around the U.S. flew in for the ceremony. As a lieutenant, I was tasked to escort one of the visiting dignitaries for the retirement ceremony. Since there were so many dignitaries coming for the ceremony, I was asked to use my personal vehicle to pick up the VIP at the flight line and drive him to the retirement ceremony at the Officer's Club. The only problem was that my 1968 Ford Mustang was in the shop for new brakes. I asked a fellow student if I could borrow his car for this task. Sure, no problem he said. His car was a Triumph TR-6 convertible with no muffler. The VIP I was to escort was the Wing Commander, Colonel Clyde Morganti, from Reese Air Force Base whom I knew a bit from my recent time at Reese Air Force Base. We made quite a spectacle as I arrived in front of the club in a cloud of dust and smoke and a very loud backfiring car. Colonel Morganti was more than pleased to ride in the convertible as he said he didn't like stuffy old staff cars any way.

I still had more training to come. My next stop was Homestead Air Force Base near Miami, Florida for an intense water survival training course. We had nearly three days of classroom training on the techniques of how to survive in the water if we ever parachuted out of our aircraft. Since most all the pilots in the class were headed to the war in Southeast Asia, we had some very intense party time each evening after the classroom instructions.

Finally, the end of the week arrived, and we were on the water to practice all we learned in the classroom. The most exciting portion of the training was parasailing and landing in the water under a full parachute. We were each strapped into a harness and then towed behind a boat up to one hundred feet above the water. The person on the back of the boat would wave two green flags which told us to release the tow line and start our descent into the water. We were to release our survival equipment bag and life raft, and then "maneuver" our parachute to a safe water landing. Once in the water we were to climb into our survival raft and attempt to utilize some of our survival equipment—the survival radio, signaling devices, and water bailing techniques. Since there was always a helicopter circling the drop area looking for sharks, I am convinced that I barely got wet hitting the water and immediately got into my survival raft. It was a very fun week in the hot Florida sun.

Finally, it was time to learn how to fly the airplane that I would pilot for twelve months in the war in Southeast Asia. Our Cessna 0-2A Skymaster training would take place at Hurlburt Field in the panhandle of Florida near Fort Walton Beach. Ten of us started the class in early November 1970. We began in a ground school environment that included classes in aircraft systems, map reading, rules of engagement (ROE), the law of armed conflict, weather, and navigation systems, and some very basic simulator training in a Link Trainer. I had an awakening during my first simulator ride. The simulator instructor was a Staff Sergeant, but he was wearing the wings of an Air Force Command pilot. I questioned him about the obvious disconnect as all pilots in the Air Force were commissioned officers. He told me that he had been passed over for promotion to Major and was just biding his time as a Staff Sergeant until he could retire with twenty years of service.

Since the airfield at Hurlburt was so congested, primarily with large C-130 Hercules transport aircraft, all of our flight training took place at an auxiliary airfield, Holley Field, that was located about ten miles west-northwest of Hurlburt. There was a bus that could take us to the airfield for our flying, but most of us just drove our own vehicles to the airfield. The airfield had two runways: 09/27 and 17/35, and each was 3,600 feet long. I had not flown a propeller-driven airplane since my fist month in pilot training at Reese Air Force Base, but I didn't think it would be a big deal to fly the 0-2A.

The 0-2A was a converted civilian aircraft, the Cessna 337, specifically modified for the FAC mission. The 0-2A was thirty-feet long, with a thirty-eight-foot wingspan, a maximum weight of 5,400 pounds, and maximum speed of 200 miles per hour. It had two Continental IO-36, 210-horsepower engines mounted in a centerline thrust arrangement. It was configured with one engine in the front and one engine in the back of the aircraft. The airplane was affectionately known as the Oscar Duck because of the way the gear would come up on takeoff; it was also widely known as the Suck and Blow aircraft.

The 0-2A had two hard points under each wing, a MAU-3A pylon, that could accommodate the SUU-11A mini-gun pod, LAU-59A Rocket Launchers, or a variety of flares. The most amazing feature was the very complex array of radios and navigation aids. The aircraft had two frequency modulation (FM) radios, two very high frequency (VHF) radios, two ultra high frequency (UHF) radios, and a high frequency (HF) radio. These radios would be the lifeline of the FAC during the war. In addition, it had a tactical navigation (TACAN) receiver, a VHF omnidirectional range (VOR) receiver, and a very ancient automatic direction finder (ADF) system. This archaic system would be a life saver for flying into very remote airfields in Southeast Asia.

The aircraft also had a weapons selector panel and a very rudimentary gun sight to assist with munition launches. The gun sight was mostly ineffective, and we usually relied on a grease pencil mark on the wind screen for very accurate munition launches.

We barely became proficient in the use of the armament system as our primary goal at Holley Field was to ensure we could first fly the airplane, second operate all the radios, and finally control an aircraft delivering ordnance during daylight and nighttime operations. Approximately ten hours of flight instruction was concentrated on flying the airplane, using the navigation aids, and reading a map. The next twenty hours of the thirty-hour training program was learning to employ the 0-2A as a FAC aircraft.

We flew to the gunnery range at England Air Force Base in Louisiana for both day and night control of A-37 Dragonfly aircraft dropping bombs on the targets that I had identified. At night we used a combination of log markers and flares to give us enough visual clues to safely control the ordnance drops. I was never very comfortable doing night FAC missions but would find out during the war that night missions would become fairly routine.

While all of the aircraft and introductory training was preparing me for the war, we had some other rather mundane things, I thought at the time, we needed to get accomplished before we left for Southeast Asia. We had to update our wills and next of kin information, banking information for our monthly pay, and various other administrative things like fingerprints, dog tags, dental work, and flight physicals. One area that kicked our butts was the necessary inoculations that were required before we headed to Southeast Asia. In other words, we had to get a whole bunch of shots. In the infinite wisdom of the Air Force they gave each one of us all eight required shots at the same time. The vaccines were loaded in an air gun and each one of us walked through the line to get the massive shot in our right arms. Those shots included typhoid, tetanus, polio, flu, plague, yellow fever, hepatitis C, and smallpox. Needless to say, our entire training class was put on Duty Not Including Flying (DNIF) status for the next four days, from November 26 to November 29, 1970. I remember just lying in my bed in the Bachelor Offices Quarters (BOQ) freezing and sweating profusely for two solid days. What a way to enter a war.

So finally, on December 10, 1970, I was certified as a fully qualified, stateside, 0-2A Forward Air Controller and began my journey to Vietnam. I was able to spend a few days driving to my home in Portland, Oregon and soon enough was on my way to Travis Air Force Base in California, just outside San Francisco. I checked into the Bachelor Officer's Quarters (BOQ) at Travis and then did some more important out processing. I basically had to review all the final paperwork that I had completed at Hurlburt Field in Florida. I got my flight information that I would be departing Travis on December 29 in a commercial Boeing 707 on my way to the Philippines for my next great adventure, Jungle Survival. We had a nearly four-hour layover in Tokyo, Japan, but we were not permitted to leave the passenger lounge.

There were 215 of us on our way to the war. A lot of Army troops were also on the chartered Boeing 707 aircraft, and we were packed in like sardines. I look back now and am amazed that each one of us had our full name, rank, and social security number in very large writing printed on the outside of our personal canvas bags. The bags held very few personal items, mostly my flying gear and personal toiletries. After what seemed like an incredibly long flight, we arrived at Manila International Airport on December 31, 1970. All of the passengers heading to the Pacific Air Forces (PACAF) Jungle Survival School boarded a bus and started our trip to Clark Air Force Base.

Since it was News Year's Eve, there was plenty of partying going on as I headed to the Officer's Club for a few beers. Due to the jet lag from the trip, I was barely able to make it to midnight to welcome in 1971. Once back in my quarters, I had the strangest thing happen. During the night I heard what I was convinced was someone in my room was saying "F**k you." I nearly crapped my pants hearing that call and thinking another drunk pilot had entered my room. I peeled my eyes open and then tried to go back to sleep. I heard that call throughout the rest of the night. I thought it was just another pilot that was very drunk from the New Year's Eve party. In the morning when I went back to the club for breakfast, I asked a fellow FAC, Ed Hooker, if he heard the person calling out during the night. He laughed and told me he had been briefed about a very special type of lizard that ate bugs in the BOQ and made a call that sounded like "F**k you." The real name of the FU lizard is a Tokay Gecko that can grow up to twenty inches long. They are completely nocturnal and are known to bite humans. Hence, I was introduced to the infamous "F**k you" lizard of Southeast Asia.

Since it was New Year's Day, we had no classes and I just laid around to catch up on my sleep in preparation for a two-week long survival school. Even though I heard the FU lizard throughout the next few nights, I was so exhausted I slept through all the future gecko calls.

The classroom portion of the training was fast and furious, covering many topics, some similar to the basic survival school in Washington state but some specific to survival in the jungle environment. We learned how to locate a safe source of drinking water, the kinds of food we could eat and, just as important, the kinds we couldn't eat. We learned how to use our survival radios, how to do field medical procedures, and how to use a jungle penetrator if required to be hoisted out of the jungle. One very unique tool that we learned about was a device that we could use to lower ourselves out of a tree if our parachutes were caught up in the branches. I never really got a straight answer on how long the device was or how far you could descend without running out of cord.

Additional training showed us how to conceal our equipment and ourselves and how to evade the enemy if necessary. One scary part of the training, at least to me, was the demonstration of all the various poisonous and non-poisonous snakes that were in the jungle. In my estimation every snake was poisonous and needed to be avoided. The Jungle Survival School had a pet mascot for the school, a ginormous Python called Charlie. If I remember correctly, the snake was seventeen feet long and weighed 184 pounds. The instructors showed us how they fed Charlie with a couple of live chickens. I was sure glad Charlie was housed in a very large enclosed compound and hoped I would never face a creature like Charlie once I got into the jungles of Vietnam. You will read about a real snake story later in these memories.

The field portion of the training was very intense as we were to demonstrate our classroom knowledge in a three-day field exercise. Our instructors showed us many techniques on how to use each piece of the survival equipment that we would carry in our survival vests. We had a single night in the jungle where we each had to construct a minimal shelter and spend the night sleeping in that structure. Needless to say, I didn't sleep much that night as I was certain that every nasty animal in the jungle would come by at some time and try to eat me.

Following that exciting night, we embarked on an escape and evasion exercise where we would have about a one-hour lead to go into the jungle and conceal ourselves. The trick was our "enemy" that was trying to find us were local indigenous natives called Negritos that were hired by the Air Force to track us down. If they did find us, they were given a ten-pound bag of rice for each student they found. I thought I had a perfect hiding place in amongst the thick underbrush. The only thing I found was a whole "herd" of very pissed off ants that started biting every place on my body that was not covered up. I was so happy when the Negrito found me. I would have gladly given him an extra bag of rice if he had found me thirty minutes earlier. Little did I know that some members of our class knew all about this exercise beforehand and hid in plain sight so they could be found and sent back to the gathering site as there were no penalties for being "captured." When this exercise was completed, we were all bused back to the base and prepared to leave the Philippines and fly to Vietnam.

After it was determined that our flight to Vietnam would be delayed one day, a few of the FACs decided it was time to see the city. So just outside the main gate of Clark Air Force Base was a Jeepney stand. A Jeepney was a converted U.S. Army WWII Jeep that the locals had converted to a kind of taxi to move folks around. The back of the Jeepney was open air and you had to hang on for dear life trying not to get thrown out as the driver speed the three miles or so into the heart of Angeles City. We asked him to take us to the closest bar in the city. I don't remember the name of the bar, but it was full of military folks of all ranks.

We were warned not to eat the local food, so we just stayed with a local beer; I think it was called Hilli or something like that. It was cold and tasted very refreshing in the very oppressive heat and humidity that was at a level I had never experienced. What we weren't advised of was the local beer had formaldehyde as a preservative. I had the worst hang over the next morning for my flight to Vietnam. It was lucky that I didn't lose the beer and all my food on my next flight from the Philippines to Vietnam.

Chapter 4
FINALLY ARRIVED AT THE WAR

Our flight into Cam Rhan Bay, South Vietnam was in a C-130 with the very uncomfortable web seating. It was hot and humid on the flight, something that I never really got used to during the entire year in Vietnam. Cam Rhan was located on the east coast of Vietnam on the South China Sea. Once we landed, we were put on a bus and taken to the air terminal and checked in with transportation for our next destination.

I was assigned to 504th Tactical Air Support Group but knew I would probably be sent to another location for my final unit assignment. When I arrived at the 504th location, I had more in-processing to complete and more paperwork to fill out. We were given an in-country indoctrination briefing on the culture of the Vietnamese people, some safety precautions, and a bunch of other stuff of questionable value. I was finally told that I would be assigned to Bien Hoa Air Force Base, about sixteen miles from Saigon, and I was assigned to the 19th Tactical Air Support Squadron (TASS). I still did not know the exact Army unit that I would be supporting. In typical military fashion, there would not be a flight available to Bien Hoa until the next morning. I think I just hung out in the barracks that evening, got a meal at the Officer's Club, and contemplated what the heck I was doing so far from home.

The morning flight was right on schedule, and I flew to Bien Hoa in C-7 Caribou airplane: web seats, hot and humid, and more jet fuel fumes than I thought were safe. We arrived at Bien Hoa in mid-morning and for the first time someone from the squadron met me at the airplane and drove me and my bag to the operations building of the 19th TASS in an open-air Jeep. What a relief as the operations building was air conditioned and had a large refrigerator that was filled with soft drinks and very cold beer. Once again, there was more paperwork to be filled out, verified, and signed. The staff sergeant that in processed me told me I would be a FAC for the 25th Infantry Division, would have a call sign of Issue 22 and would be flying out of Bien Hoa.

He assigned me a room in one of the FAC hooches where another FAC unit was housed. My initial room assignment was to a "visiting" FAC room. Bunk beds with a small shared closet were the only amenities that we had. Since I had very little personal stuff, that was no problem as I wasn't at the hooch that much. I was the newest FAC in the building, so I ended up on the top bunk. I don't really remember who the bottom bunkmate was as he was just transiting through Bien Hoa waiting for his final FAC assignment.

The hooch had a very large center great room with numerous sofas, tables, a poker table, and best of all a hooch bar with a very large and loud refrigerator where we could imbibe on our favorite alcoholic and nonalcoholic beverages. Adjacent to the great room was a large bathroom with six sinks and six showers that was basically a communal area for all the occupants of the hooch. The hooch had twelve rooms laid out on either side of the great room with a long narrow hall down the middle. Some of the senior FACs had rooms to themselves including our squadron flight surgeon and a couple of air liaison officers (ALO).

Outside of the great room was a concrete patio that held our very dilapidated barbecue grill. I was eventually assigned to a permanent room that I shared with an OV-10 Rash FAC, Ron Russing. Having my own room was nice but I didn't get to use it much after I was assigned to a different FAC unit because I was deployed to the field for seven days at a time and then would return for two nights back to Bien Hoa before flying to the remote site for another seven days. My room at Bien Hoa would eventually change to a permanent room at Tan Son Nhut Air Force Base in Saigon and in Ban Me Thuot, South Vietnam.

Following my room assignment, I stopped by the military pay section to make sure my finances were in order and my bank information for payment was correct. I also had to exchange some of my U.S. dollars for MPC, or military pay certificates. U.S. Troops used the MPC for financial transactions in Vietnam. MPCs were paper money in denominations of five cents, ten cents, twenty-five cents, fifty cents, one dollar, five dollars, ten dollars, and twenty dollars. The intent of the MPC was to keep U.S. currency out of the hands of the enemy as it was an extremely valuable asset to the North Vietnamese.

I was also introduced to the extremely well stocked Base Exchange System in Vietnam where you could buy just about anything you needed or wanted. The only exception was alcohol; we were issued an alcohol ration card giving us access to, I think, four bottles of hard alcohol a month. For me that ration card became a very strong bargaining tool as I certainly did not drink that much alcohol. One very useful feature of the Base Exchange (BX) was the very large BX catalogue system where you could by just about anything. I purchased my first 35 mm camera, a Pentax with a 50 mm lens and a 200 mm telephoto lens. This camera would be my constant companion for the rest of my tour—I took almost 2,000 photos. Since the BX had an excellent photo processing service, I had all of my 35 mm slides processed at the BX during my tour.

That first morning at the squadron was such a blur. I remember that Lieutenant Colonel William Montgomery, the squadron operations officer, met me in the flight planning room before leading me to a small office to give me my initial in-country briefing. He was none too pleased that yet another brand-new lieutenant was assigned to his squadron. He explained that he wanted me to get my combat checkout as soon as possible but that wouldn't come until I had about 125 hours of supervised combat mission time in my logbook. He also stated that there was nothing going on in this war that needed me to die for. He told me to just follow the rules of engagement (ROE) and finish my tour safely.

He then dismissed me, telling me to go to base supply and the squadron life support section to get all my required gear. He also told me that I was on the schedule for my first in-country flight the next morning and that my instructor would be an Australian Flight Lieutenant (the equivalent of a U.S.A.F. Captain) Chris Hudnot. Australia had numerous operations in place during the Vietnam War including FACs supporting many different units, a B-57 Squadron that supported air strikes throughout the entire country, a UH-1 helicopter detachment, a C-7 Caribou cargo hauling squadron and, very early in the war, a squadron of CA-27s (F-86s) based in Ubon, Thailand.

The final words from Lieutenant Colonel Montgomery during my in-country briefing were, "Now get out of here and don't kill yourself." So off I went to the base supply building to get my flying gear. I was issued two pairs of Nomex flying gloves (material that isn't supposed to burn in a fire), a pair of jungle combat boots, a flak jacket (vest) that weighed about fifteen pounds, a camouflaged poncho liner, and a very heavy rubber poncho to keep me dry in the rain. Also, for the first time I was issued two Nomex flight suits that were just coming into use in the Air Force. The supply tech directed me to a fabric shop in the same building where they would sew my rank on the new flight suits.

When all that was finished, I returned to the squadron building, by foot of course, as there were no squadron vehicles available other than the blue Flight Line Truck that took us to and from the flight line. I was starting to get excited as all the pieces were falling in place for me to get flying again. Once in the squadron Life Support Shop, I was fitted for my helmet, which was supposed to be somewhat bullet resistant. It weighed a ton and really was uncomfortable on my ears. But it was all we had available so it would have to do. Next, I was issued the personal weapons that I would fly with. First was a Smith and Wesson .38 caliber revolver and an accompanying web belt with leather holster and two additional leather pouches that would each hold six bullets. I had to sign the pistol out every time I flew and return it after each flight to be stored in the Life Support locker. I thought it was strange that we would have to return our weapon after each flight as the war could easily get to our sleeping quarters and I wanted to be armed.

In addition to the revolver, I was issued a CAR-15 rifle (Colt Automatic Rifle) with a full magazine of 5.56 mm rounds. The CAR-15 was a fully automatic rifle but was a shorter and lighter version of the standard M-16 that most U.S. troops utilized in the war. The rifle, like the pistol, had to be kept at the Life Support locker after each flight. I learned after a few days in country that most pilots did not fly with the AR-15, just the revolver. However later in this story you will see that I did fly with a Soviet made AK-47. The AK-47 was the weapon of choice of both the North Vietnamese Army (NVA) and the Vietcong (VC). The AK-47 used a 7.62 mm round and was much more durable under adverse conditions than the CAR-15.

Continuing to collect my life support gear, I was issued my own parachute. The life support technician fitted the parachute straps to my body, and I had my own life support peg to hang my gear on when not flying. Additional items included my survival vest. It weighed about ten pounds when full of all the equipment I would need in case of a survival situation. Some of the items in the vest included:

- Two survival radios
- First aid kit
- Water-proof match container
- Whistle
- Signal mirror
- Water storage bag
- Large tourniquet
- Pilot's survival knife
- USAF Survival Manual
- Tree extraction cord
- Two blood chits
- Water purification tablets
- Two smoke flares
- Two pen gun flares
- Compass

In addition, I also carried twelve extra .38 caliber bullets in my survival vest. I must explain the blood chits that we carried in our survival vest. Blood chits were used by U.S. aviators as a way of communicating with non-English speaking people. The chits that we carried were made of silk and served as a safe passage pass for a downed aviator in need of help from friendly local people. This Vietnam blood chit was printed in fourteen different languages and included the American flag and a serial number. It was used throughout Southeast Asia. The blood chit stated that the bearer of the chit was American, required assistance, and that those who helped the pilot will be rewarded for their service by the U.S. Government. How the reward would be paid in the field is still a mystery to me.

Probably one of the most useful items was the large KA-BAR survival knife that was issued along with my other survival equipment. It was just less than twelve inches long and had a seven-inch serrated blade. It was issued with a leather holder and I wore it every day I was in Vietnam because it came in handy opening C ration cans, beer cans, and anything else that needed opening. I will explain another useful purpose my knife served later in these memories.

After I collected all my combat gear, I was told to report to the fighter wing, I think it was the 3rd Tactical Fighter wing, at Bien Hoa to see the intelligence shop for a detailed update of some personal information. The intel shop needed to build a profile on every pilot flying out of Bien Hoa in case we were ever involved in a combat search and rescue situation.

The rescue force always wanted to confirm the person they were trying to rescue was actually the person they thought it was. They did not want the enemy to draw them into a trap by faking pilot information. I had to fill out a detailed information sheet on myself that included my blood type, next of kin information, existing scars, tattoos, home addresses, etc. Following this data, I also filled out another form with, I think, five personal questions that only I would know the answer to. What was your high school mascot? What was the model of your first car? What was your first home telephone number? What was the name of your first girlfriend? What is your favorite color? Following this data collection, I had my picture taken both from the front and from the side with my Social Security number printed on a long narrow board. I thought I was being booked into jail.

So, on my second day at Bien Hoa I started my check out as a FAC in the 0-2. My first flight concentrated on traffic patterns, touch and go landings, and a cross-country flight to a base at Vung Tau on the coast of Vietnam. It was good to finally be flying again and during the initial check out period I flew every single day for the rest of January and missed only two days of flying in February. I was determined to complete my combat ready check as soon as possible.

You may be wondering how I can remember all these details after so many years. Well, I did keep a very detailed diary about most of my flights and also kept my personal flying logbook up to date with times and mission descriptions. In addition to the diary and the flight logbook, I took nearly 2,000 photos (35 mm) of my activities in Southeast Asia. A review of the photos brought back some very vivid details that are shared in these memories. I will also relate at the end of these memories what happened to a very large number of those 35 mm slides.

This is a good time to explain the role of the Forward Air Controller in Southeast Asia. The FAC's mission was to fly directly above the battlefield in a small unarmed observation aircraft to find and mark enemy targets with a white phosphorus spotting rocket, to control the fighters that dropped the bombs, and to do a bomb damage assessment after each attack. The FACs expertise as an air strike controller also made him an intelligence source, munitions expert, communications expert, and above all, the on-scene commander of the strike forces and the start of any subsequent search and rescue mission if necessary. Since the FAC was assigned to a specific geographical area they became the absolute expert on what was happening in their area of responsibility (AOR). The FAC knew whenever even a blade of grass was misplaced or that some activity had taken place in their AOR.

Whenever a FAC supported U.S. troops on the ground, the FAC had to be designated an "A" FAC and have some fighter pilot qualifications. That was the designation I got by completing the Fighter Lead In program at Cannon Air Force Base in the fall of 1970. This requirement was in place to ensure there were no friendly fire incidents killing U.S. troops on the ground with an errant bomb or missile. Protecting the friendlies on the ground from the ordnance that the FAC controlled was one of the most precise and heart-stopping aspects of being a FAC.

All of the FACs in Southeast Asia really questioned this requirement as all FACs were fully qualified to conduct and direct an air strike near friendly troops… and believe me in a critical situation the U.S. troops on the ground could care less if it was an A FAC directing the attack as long as they didn't get killed in the airstrike.

The strike missions we were expected to support were either preplanned strikes (scheduled at least twenty-four hours in advance on a specific target) or an immediate airstrike when the situation on the ground needed immediate air support. In my case, I added the missions of the inserting, supporting, and extracting Special Forces teams and a very intense High Low mission that I will describe later. We could be expected to do some or all of those tasks on each mission. We flew at around 1,000 feet above the battle so we could find the targets, observe the action, and be easy target practice for the bad guys.

There was a North Vietnam and Vietcong philosophy about shooting at the FAC: the bad guys never wanted to start shooting at the FAC until the fighters were on scene. I guess they had the hope that if they didn't shoot at us it would be harder to find them. But once they knew we had detected them it was like an arcade shooting gallery. Toward the end of my time in Southeast Asia the bad guys added a very fearsome weapon, the hand-held SA-7 Strela surface-to-air, heat-seeking missile. This weapon was in addition to the AK-47 7.62 mm small arms, 12.7 mm (.51 caliber), 14.7 mm, and 37 mm. antiaircraft guns they used throughout the war.

I had many close calls and many rounds hit the aircraft I was flying. We used to call those hairy missions "seat sucking missions," which meant after we landed, we needed help from the crew chief to pull the seat cushions out of our asses. During night missions we flew with our exterior lights off to lessen the chances of being seen by the enemy and shot down. The most imminent danger during a night mission was a mid-air collision with the fighter aircraft we were controlling, which also flew with their exterior lights off. Night missions were doubly exciting as we could see the many tracers that were fired at our aircraft. The NVA/VC usually had about every fifth round as a tracer round. The tracer rounds helped them see where their fire was going but also showed us exactly where the fire was coming from. I very occasionally saw tracer rounds during day missions.

We did have a few other sophisticated techniques to keep from getting shot down: trying to make our attack with sun at our backs if the terrain and sun angle was right, flying behind a ridge line if the terrain was good, and, best of all, flying with one foot a rudder. This full-rudder deflection made us fly almost sideways to give the impression from the ground that the nose of the aircraft was tracking one way while in fact we were flying about thirty degrees off from that track. It was amazing to see the tracers track way out in front of the aircraft. Sometimes the more experienced gunners found out about our trick flying and many of my fellow pilots were shot down. We also used jinking maneuvers, which were very uncoordinated and erratic flight movements that never gave the enemy a predictable flight path that we were flying. I tried to never fly a straight flight path for more than a few seconds.

We also had one other cool technique we used to protect us. The squadron sent down a directive that told us we must to fly with our flack vests. Flying, wearing a flack vest, a survival vest, and a parachute was just too cumbersome and got in the way of flying so we would take our flack vest and place it under the aircraft seat cushion. The thought was at least we would save the family jewels if we were hit in that part of the aircraft…as the old Australian beer commercial goes: BRILLIANT. But I was still alive and felt invincible.

One other interesting bit of information I was given at my briefing was the FAC rules to follow. These edicts came from 7th Air Force in Saigon and Pacific Air Force Command (PACAF) in Hawaii, and in my mind were just a recommendation as we always needed to fly the mission to get the job done. I kept a copy of these instructions but never really looked at them again during my tour.

PACAF Tactics and Techniques Bulletins 17 and 47 described FAC tactics and techniques in a general sense. Bulletin 52 covered the problems of finding and recognizing enemy targets and combating enemy ground fire. Due to a general increase in enemy activity during 1971, this ground fire had become highly intense and accurate. Therefore, this bulletin addressed techniques for strike control and target marking emphasizing minimal exposure to ground fire and more efficient use of aircraft capabilities. An excerpt includes:

1. The FAC should perform an area reconnaissance of the target area prior to arrival of the strike aircraft, if possible, to confirm the position of friendly forces and study the target terrain, weather, etc. All operations in the target area should be at an altitude above the effective range of small arms fire (approximately 1,500 feet AGL) unless there is an urgent operational requirement to fly lower. The FAC should have a plan or system but should not establish a set pattern. He should take advantage of sun, clouds, speed, binoculars, etc., to protect and separate himself from the enemy. Actual communications with the strike aircraft and basic FAC procedures are outlined in PACAFM 55-01. Concise, accurate briefings and limited radio usage will greatly enhance the effectiveness of the strike and safety of friendly forces involved.

2. In the target area, the strike pilots and FAC should keep each other in sight as much as possible, especially in areas of restricted terrain clearance

or during periods of marginal visibility due to weather or darkness. The FAC should always insure the strike aircraft have him in sight and are ready to attack prior to his marking the target.

   a. The primary purpose of the FAC's mark is to provide a clearly visible, common reference point for the FAC and strike pilots. The technique of accurately marking a target, while important, is not so vital that FAC position, vulnerability to ground fire or strike effectiveness should be compromised.

   b. The actual mark may be a rocket with white phosphorus or high explosive head, a colored smoke grenade, tracer rounds from a hand-held weapon, or any object dropped from the aircraft which contrasts with the surrounding terrain and can be seen by the strike pilots.

   c. Target marking may also be accomplished by the ground forces using colored signal panels, signal mirrors, tracer cross-fire, smoke grenades, balloons, smoke generators or artillery/mortar smoke rounds. Natural and man-made terrain features and objects may also be used to describe the target location. Any time colored smoke is used for target marking, the color should not be revealed over the radio until the smoke has become visible to preclude the enemy from using diversionary smoke of the same color.

3. The techniques of target marking will be influenced by the type of mark, target terrain, weather, type and perishability of target, ground fire, and FAC experience and ability.

   a. The FAC must know the type of target he has and mark accordingly. A mark directly on an enemy troop concentration will cause them to disperse and will degrade the effectiveness of the strike, whereas an offset mark will give a common reference point and not alert the enemy. Bridges, sampans, trucks, and other more or less stationary targets, in or near trees or camouflaged, should be marked directly since they will most likely be difficult for the strike pilot to see.

   b. The FAC should always give the strike pilots any restrictions to attack and breakaway headings such as friendly troop positions, terrain, weather, borders, etc., and offer recommended attack and breakaway headings based on these restrictions. Generally, the best direction of attack is parallel to friendly lines because of the possibility of hung ordnance or runaway guns. Consideration should also be given to known enemy ground fire, obstacles and pilots' visibility of the target. The flight leader should make the final decision on the attack heading, but the FAC should not hesitate to halt the strike should the direction of attack jeopardize the safety of friendly troops or aircraft.

4. The FAC normally has several methods of marking the target and should use the one that best fits the situation.

   a. A good technique for marking a target with rockets is to position the target off the wingtip, confirm that the strike pilots have the FAC in sight, roll in and turn toward the target using coordinated control movements and arming the rocket as the nose passes down; through the horizon. Then, line up quickly on the target, insure the aircraft is still in coordinated flight, and fire the rocket. Recover above 1,500 feet AGL. Make: a coordinated, maximum effort pull-up away from the target, maintain good airspeed and disarm the rockets as the nose passes up through the horizon. Observe the point of impact and quickly give corrections from the mark to the target. Take up a position to observe the ordnance delivery and keep clear of the strike aircraft. The FAC is most vulnerable to ground fire when at low speeds near a stall, following a set pattern or pointed directly at the target in a dive. Avoid these situations as much as possible. Accurate rocket travel is due largely to coordinated aircraft control at launch and good sighting techniques. The rockets should be sighted like a shotgun using the sighting rod, if installed, for lateral sighting and a spot on the windscreen about eye and rocket tube level for vertical sighting. Learn to fire quickly once the aircraft is pointed at the target to limit exposure to ground fire.

   b. A diving delivery of a hand-held object, such as a smoke grenade or cloth marker, is made in much the same manner as rocket delivery. Align the target under the wing and roll in toward the target, dive as steeply as possible, align the nose of the aircraft with the target and release quickly. Recover as in a rocket: delivery.

   c. Level delivery of a hand-held object is best done by an observer from the rear or right seat with the left seat pilot calling the drop as the target disappears under the wing while flying directly over the target. Objects can be dropped from the left seat using the same sighting techniques. Any objects dropped should be kept "safe" until outside the aircraft, i.e. pull pins on grenades outside the cockpit and throw objects away from the aircraft. Do not drop fused incendiary or explosive objects from the aircraft unless fusing will allow safe separation.

   d. If it becomes necessary to mark a target with tracers, again it is best done by an observer from the right seat. Most small arms will have a slight drop from 1,500 feet so aim above and behind the target, fire a short burst and correct the aiming point. Firing hand-held weapons is recommended only as a last resort.

5. As in all phases of flight, it is extremely important to use smooth throttle technique during target marking. Jamming the throttle forward during marking, in orbit during the strike, or during the bomb damage assessment (BDA), could result in engine stoppage in a very dangerous area.

6. The FAC is responsible for avoiding mid-air collisions in the target area; therefore, he should ensure that he has the strike aircraft in sight or that they see him at all times, especially during ordnance delivery passes. Keep the strike aircraft advised of other known aircraft and artillery fire in the area.

7. The same aircraft control techniques apply during the BDA and it is advisable to keep a running BDA as the strike progresses and complete the BDA before the strike aircraft depart the area. Hits from small arms have been reported above 1,500 feet AGL so don't put the aircraft in a vulnerable position at any altitude. If mission accomplishment requires operations at a lower altitude, remember that the greater your airspeed, the quicker you will fly out of the range of ground fire. Sinking and uncoordinated flight will adversely affect the gunners' aim but will also slow down your exit from the area.

In addition to all these FAC procedural rules, we were also "restrained" by the Law of Armed Conflict (LAC) and a specific set of rules of engagement (ROE) that we also had to follow. I did get a very short introductory Law of Armed Conflict briefing upon my arrival in Vietnam, but I don't believe I ever received a formal ROE briefing. I learned the specific ROE with on-the-job training as I was checked out as a combat ready FAC.

The basic premise of the LAC was to regulate the conduct of armed forces to protect the fundamental human rights of those involved in the conflict. The ROE directives were meant to describe the exact circumstances under which I could employ any of the fire power available to me as a FAC.

Rules of Engagement (ROE) were directive in nature and compliance was required by all U.S. military forces carrying out activities in the war. Supplementing these rules, and usually more restrictive, were operating rules and policies established by the Commander of the 7th Air Force. The ROE formally stated what was permitted or forbidden in air operations. These ROE came directly to me from 7th Air Force; however, the ROE was usually specifically outlined and approved by the Secretary of Defense and ultimately approved by the President. The ROE delineated when, where, how, and against whom military force could be used and the implications if we didn't follow them.

Now being a lieutenant in my early twenties, it was obvious to me that there were just too many political implications attached to our ROE. Were we trying to win this war or were we just fooling around? Whenever we found a target of interest there was much contemplation whether the target fit all the criteria of the ROE. For targets in Cambodia and, I assume, South Vietnam, there was also the approval process of the local chief who either approved or stopped an attack on a specific target.

The rules for the fighters that attacked North Vietnam were even more restrictive and really stupid. For example, we couldn't bomb any enemy supplies in port, couldn't bomb any airfields, and couldn't shoot down enemy airplanes while they were in the airfield's landing pattern. In addition, many years after the war, it was revealed that all U.S. bombing routes into North Vietnam were secretly announced to the enemy before each bombing mission. We lost many brave people because of the stupidity of our government.

One area that did give us some specific ROE guidance was that the Buddhist Temples that were located all over Cambodia were absolutely off limits for any attack. The VC and the NVA knew these restrictions well and would almost daily shoot at us or the fighters from the temples, since they knew we could not respond.

I do remember one attack I was controlling near the Cambodian town of Kratie. We were taking fire from a temple on almost every target run as we were striking a supply point about 300 meters from the temple. I gave specific instructions to the fighters to avoid the temple but that we were taking heavy ground fire from the same temple. During one attack a South Vietnamese (SVN) F-5 fighter dropped one 500-pound bomb that just happened to hit the front door of the temple. Oh well, the fog of war. Fortunately, since a few NVA soldiers were killed in the temple, the NVA never reported the incident as that would have broken the ROE that the NVA/VC were also "required" to follow.

One key distinction of the ROE for the FAC was that the FAC, no matter what rank, had the ultimate responsibility and final authority for the safe conduct of any bombing mission conducted by U.S. forces. Many times, the FAC, including me, would send the U.S. fighters off station as they were stretching the bounds of the ROE with the inaccuracy of their bombs. I can remember I was controlling a flight of four F-4 fighters while I was still an Issue FAC in South Vietnam. After the first pass the fighters dropped their bombs nearly 200 meters from where I had marked the target. With ground troops nearby, I just could not take the chance of dropping the bombs on our troops, known as a friendly fire incident.

There was another ROE situation where the ROE allowed almost unrestricted bombing. This situation was known as a "free-fire zone." We were authorized to attack any target with any weapon at any time as the area was known to contain only enemy forces or enemy supply sites and there would be no friendlies in the area. These free-fire zones didn't happen very often, and I only saw a few of them in Cambodia.

So, this was the mission that I was being checked out to do. The training flights were intense and included many visual reconnaissance missions to get to know every square inch of my AOR. Practice launches of my spotting rockets, 2.75-inch folding fin white phosphorous rockets, were challenging but also a fun part of the check out. The 0-2 had a gunsight mounted on the left side of the windscreen that was marginal at best. Chris Hudnot, the Australian lieutenant, showed me an amazing technique for shooting very accurate rockets. He made a ¼-inch grease pencil mark on the inside of the windscreen and used that as his gun sight. The seat height was a critical factor in the use of the grease mark on the windscreen. You had to have the seat height adjusted exactly the same for your own sitting height. In addition to the grease mark, he showed me a very critical part of the formula for getting rockets on target every time and that was an incredibly steep dive angle to the target. His technique, that I also adopted, was to pull the nose of the aircraft up to almost vertical, step on one of the rudders and "turn" the aircraft almost vertically to the ground. It was a very effective technique; I won many a beer in rocket shooting contests with other FACs in my unit and accurately marked many targets.

Controlling the fighters dropping the bombs was also a challenging task. Keeping sight of the fighters, keeping the target on the ground in sight, keeping track of the friendlies on the ground, and talking on the correct radio was a challenge all in itself. As I described the O-2 earlier, we had a wide array of radios. We could listen to all of them at once but had to select the specific radio to talk on during the battle. The ground troops would be on an FM channel, the fighters would be on a UHF Channel, the Army attack helicopters would be on a VHF channel, and sometimes an Army command and control helicopter would be on a second FM channel. So, it was a real "goat rope" experience to make sure you had the correct channel selected to talk to the correct person.

This was hard enough during the daylight to keep track of everyone without running into the fighter or attack helicopters, dropping the bombs on the wrong target, and, all the while, dodging enemy ground fire. Doing this at night was exponentially more difficult—throw in a parachute-controlled flare we dropped from our aircraft that gave us just enough light to see the target or a log flare that glowed when it hit the ground and we had our hands full conducting night airstrikes. The log flare was a magnesium-cored piece of pinewood with an internal striking mechanism. As the log flare was dropped from the aircraft the magnesium would ignite and the log would burn for up to thirty minutes whether it fell to the ground or into the water. The burning log would provide a visual marker for the FAC to direct and control munitions drops. I never really got comfortable controlling night strikes, but it was part of the FAC mission and happened at least five or six times a month.

Finally, after conducting many day and night airstrikes with Chris Hudnot in the right seat, I was declared combat ready March 24, 1971, after a little more than one hundred hours of combat time. Many of those hours were solo and on visual reconnaissance (VR) flights getting to know my AOR. I could tell if there had been any activity in any portion of the AOR by closely comparing what I saw yesterday to what I saw on the current flight. That was a trait that all the FACs in Southeast Asia became very proficient at and was a great source of actionable intelligence to support the ground troops to whom we were assigned.

Part of this VR work included how to read a map so we could pass exact coordinates to the ground troops. Preparing a map and map reading were tasks that all FACs had to master. Remember this was before the advent of the Global Positioning Satellite system (GPS). Many hours were spent on the ground compiling and cataloguing our maps. It was not unusual to have nearly 200 maps in our map cases that we took with us on every single flight. My maps were broken down into sectors. Each sector had a very recognizable landmark somewhere in the sector and was marked on plastic-covered 1:1,000,000 master map. Then I had 8 1:100,000 maps for each sector and then 2:1:50,000 maps for that particular 1:100.000 map. The map scale meant that for each one inch on the map there was a corresponding number of inches on the ground. For example, the 1:100,000 maps meant that every inch on the map meant 100,000 inches on the ground.

My indexing system was quite simple: I had the sectors marked on the very large 1:1,000,000 map A through M. Then I had each 1:100,000 map marked A1 through A8 and then had the 1:50,000 maps marked A1A through A1B. That gave me 181 maps to use for every possible mission I would fly in my AOR. I also had to be able to get to the correct map while flying the airplane, talking to people on the ground and in the air, and dodging ground fire all at the same time.

On the day of my combat ready check, March 25, 1971, I had to endure the standard new Combat Ready (CR) FAC initiation. Once the flying day was over and I was back in the FAC hooch, the other combat-veteran FACs prepared a special drink for me to commemorate my coming of age as a fully qualified combat ready FAC. The drink was no less that a whole bunch of alcohol poured into an empty 105 mm howitzer shell casing. If I remember correctly, the casing was about fifteen inches long and about four and a half inches wide. The casing was filled with just about anything we had in the hooch bar…mostly beer but also lots of various alcoholic beverages. We had to stand in front of the veteran FACs and chug the entire contents of the casing. Needless to say, I was very inebriated following that initiation and after retching a few times, I tried to get some sleep before an early morning flight.

The next morning, I was still very hung over but still got airborne and, about forty-five minutes into my flight, I became very airsick from all the alcohol from the night before. Rather than continue in a very unsafe condition, I pulled a few circuit breakers and air aborted my flight before I killed myself. I know the crew chief knew what was going on, but he didn't say a word, he just cleaned up the puke and pushed the circuit breakers back in and signed the airplane off as Code 1, or flyable. I never did that trick again in my remaining ten months of combat flying. It was just too dangerous, and I remember my Operations Officer telling me "don't kill yourself" in this war.

Following my combat check, I continued to fly every single day in support of the 25th Infantry Division, but I knew their operations were starting to wind down as the airstrikes became less frequent and the number of ground operations began to draw down. I was waiting for a new assignment to a different unit as I heard that the 25th Infantry Division would be pulling out of Vietnam and returning to their home base of operations in Hawaii.

One afternoon after returning from a flight, one of the fairly senior FAC Captains, Bob Johnson, asked me to come down to his room. Once there he told me he heard the Issue FACs would be changing support to other units and that he would like me to join his unit, the Pretzel FACs. I asked where the Pretzel FACs flew out of and who they supported. He very bluntly told me he could not tell me anything about the mission or the location of the Pretzel operations as it was a highly classified mission. He also said it was one of the most challenging and exciting FAC missions in Southeast Asia. The only way I could know about what the mission was and where it was located was to agree to join the Pretzel team. It seemed like a strange way to run a war, but it also sounded interesting to me and I said, "Sign me up." Bob still would not tell me what the mission was but said he and I would fly to a forward operating base called Quan Loi in the morning, and I would get the full briefing on the mission I was about to undertake.

Chapter 5
QUAN LOI, THE GARDEN SPOT IN SOUTHEAST ASIA

On the morning of April 5, 1971, Bob and I flew to Quan Loi. Bob was in the left seat as he said it was a little tricky landing at Quan Loi. Besides being an uncontrolled airfield, the U.S. Army had an artillery battery just to the southeast of the runway. Sometimes they would remember to announce a warning before firing off their 155 mm howitzers, and sometimes they forgot. I was now flying under the call sign Pretzel 06. Quan Loi was about sixty air miles from Bien Hoa and about five miles from the border with Cambodia. The runway was compacted dirt, 3,800 feet long, and right in the middle of an old French rubber plantation. There was no control tower, no navigation aids, and no airfield lighting at the airfield.

As we landed, I realized this was really a forward operating base with very few amenities. I was met at the aircraft by my Air Liaison Officer (ALO), Major Ron House, and two U.S. Army majors. An ALO, usually a mid to senior Air Force major, was assigned to each Army ground unit to provide tactical air advice and to facilitate communication and operational effectiveness. All three of them were wearing a special identification badge and were covered in a fine layer of red dust. The helicopters hovering at the airfield at Quan Loi put massive amounts of red dust in the air, covering everything that was outside. I will talk about the actual conditions at Quan Loi later in this story.

We all piled into two Army Jeeps and proceeded along a very dusty and bumpy road right into the middle of the rubber plantation. As we approached the compound, we were met by an indigenous-looking Montagnard, affectionately known as Yards by the U.S. troops. The Yards were Malayan/Polynesian ethic tribesmen living in the central highlands of South Vietnam. They were excellent fighters, capable and loyal. The term Yard included any one or more of several distinct tribes living in the area. The Yard guard waved us into the compound, and we all entered an underground bunker that was dug right in the middle of the compound.

As soon as we got inside, Major House welcomed me to the center of all Pretzel operations. I was really intrigued by the secrecy of the compound and could hardly wait to find out what the heck I had gotten myself into agreeing to become a Pretzel FAC.

I soon found out what I would be doing for the next nine months of my tour in Southeast Asia. I was informed that I would be flying in support of a program called The Military Assistance Command (MACV) Studies and Observation Group (SOG) or MACVSOG. U.S. Military Assistance Command, Vietnam (MACV) was a joint-service command of the U.S. Department of Defense. MACV was created on February 8, 1962, in response to the increase in U.S. military assistance to South Vietnam.

The mission of the SOG group, and the Pretzels in particular, was to support the insert, control, and extract of small Special Forces teams into Cambodia and Laos. These teams were made up of U.S. and Vietnamese Special Forces, indigenous troops—both Montagnard and Cambodian Special Forces—and had a wide variety of missions they were responsible for. In 1971 the U.S. was attempting to teach the SVN Army Special Forces to do the SOG mission on their own and some of the missions were conducted entirely by the SVN SF and indigenous forces.

On these particular SVN SF missions, we carried a Vietnamese translator who could communicate with the teams on the ground. It was always a challenge taking someone in your cockpit that barely spoke English and usually got airsick on each and every flight. Some of those missions included covert area reconnaissance, traffic watching, capture of enemy forces, destruction of enemy supplies, and, in some cases, assassination of key NVA or VC leaders. SOG's activities were intended to counter North Vietnam's use of Laos and Cambodia as vast staging areas and supply routes that were supposedly immune from attack.

Since the U.S. government denied we had any troops in Cambodia and Laos, even as a Lieutenant I could see why this mission was so classified. Following the initial briefing from Major House and the Special Forces troops, I was required to sign a Non-Disclosure Agreement that I would not tell anyone about the mission we were doing from Quan Loi for the next twenty-five years. Wow, I really was in a spooky business.

Before I get into the specifics of some of our missions, I must describe Quan Loi. As I said earlier, Quan Loi was located about five miles from the Cambodia border with South Vietnam. The runway was only 3,800 feet long, made of compacted dirt called laterite, and did not have a control tower or navigational aids on the airfield. The laterite had very high levels of iron oxide which gave the dust at Quan Loi the distinctively rusty red color. At one time there were runway lights for nighttime operations, but over the years the locals stole all the copper wires from the runway lighting system. Not having lights did not stop any of the Pretzel flying operations. We operated out of the airfield 24/7.

Our navigation procedures flying into Quan Loi in bad weather conditions were archaic at best. As we returned to Quan Loi in bad weather or in the dark, we would fly at about 2,500 feet to get a reading on the TACAN station at Bien Hoa, which was about 60 miles to the south of Quan Loi. This initial positioning would get us in the general vicinity of Quan Loi and then we would descend to around 700 to 1,000 feet, depending on the weather. The field elevation at Quan Loi was 508 feet above sea level, so the 700 to 1,000 feet would be 200 to 500 feet above the airfield. We would then request one of our maintenance troops to get in a jeep, park near the runway and turn on one of the portable Automatic Direction Finding (ADF) radios. We would then use our ADF system in the aircraft to follow the homing signal to the ADF radio on the ground.

Once the person on the ground with the radio heard us overhead, they would call us on the radio, and we would start our descent to around one hundred feet, do a 270-degree turn and hope we could pick up sight of the runway environment. One way we enhanced our chances was the crew chief in the Pretzel jeep would park at the end of the runway with the jeep lights on full bright to give us a fairly decent reference that we were going to touch down on the runway and not in the jungle.

Many times I hoped like hell that I was really lined up on the Quan Loi runway. It was such a relief to see those jeep lights and know I had dodged another bullet in my flying career. Checking my flight record, I had twenty-three night missions into Quan Loi with many more night landings in Bien Hoa, Ban Me Thuot, Phan Rang, and Saigon.

There were very minimal maintenance facilities at Quan Loi to keep our aircraft flying. We had two CONEX buildings, large ocean-going steel shipping containers, on the flight line that housed all the necessary spare aircraft parts, tools, and some of the lubricant for the aircraft. There was a third CONEX building that housed the pilot's parachutes and survival gear. We got our aviation gas from a small Army aviation contingent that had large rubber bladders for our fuel.

Our crew chiefs lived at Quan Loi and were the very best troops in the Air Force. There wasn't a thing they couldn't fix in the field. Our white phosphorus (Willy

Peete) rockets, flechette rockets, and high-explosive rockets were also supplied by the Army. We had an endless supply of the rockets. Very seldom did any of the Pretzel FACs return to Quan Loi with unexpended rockets.

The normal routine was for a Pretzel FAC to fly an 0-2 from Bien Hoa and stay at Quan Loi for seven days before returning the aircraft back to Bien Hoa for more extensive aircraft maintenance. Each pilot had a room in the barracks at Bien Hoa, and we normally stayed just two nights and one full day at Bien Hoa before going out on another seven-day deployment. We normally flew a mission inbound to Bien Hoa, then a mission after leaving Bien Hoa and recovered at Quan Loi.

It was not unusual for each one of the pilots to come up on the maximum flying time allowed by the squadron in a one-month period (one hundred hours). The edict would come down from the squadron headquarters that we could not log any more hours until the start of the new month. So, us bright lieutenants still flew, we just did not log the time in our personal file. We did log the time for the maintenance records.

Once we left the Quan Loi airfield for the SOG compound we had to deal with the very bumpy dirt road, which was carved out in the middle of the rubber plantation, and, more importantly, the red mud when it rained or the red dust when it was dry. And did it ever rain, especially during the annual monsoon season in Southeast Asia. The normal monsoon season is June to October. When the rains came it was nearly impossible to walk to and from the hooch and to the flight line. The mud would build up on your boots and make a real mess inside the airplanes. The dirt runway was as slick as snot whenever it rained very heavily, which was daily during the five-month monsoon season.

The pilots, the radio operators, and maintenance troops were all housed in a very rustic building called the Air Force hooch. The upper sides of the walls were covered in a fine mesh mosquito netting while the lower half of the walls were made of wood (from ammunition pallets) and fortified with fifty-five-gallon oil barrels and sandbags. We had a metal roof over our heads while the floor was just red dirt. We did have electricity to the building via an ancient Army generator that worked sometimes. We had power for some portable fans, and a very old refrigerator.

We did have a hot water heater in the building, but it had no power or water source and it acted as our scoreboard recording the dates and number of rocket attacks that hit our compound or runway. Every time a rocket hit Quan Loi we would add that event to the side of our water heater with a grease pencil. The total number of rocket attacks reached into the hundreds, but the actual total number was lost when the Air Force hooch was hit in September 1971 and the water heater was destroyed.

We had an old aircraft fuel tank rigged up outside our building that served as our shower. Despite the oppressive heat in Southeast Asia, the water in fuel tank was never warm. If you decided to take a shower you had to do it right out in the open, as the only semblance of a shower pan was a couple of wooden pallets laid in the mud. Most of the pilots would go the entire seven days without a shower. We knew it was time to go back to Bien Hoa when our fight suits stood up all by themselves.

There were a couple of old beat up couches and easy chairs in the main room for us to relax after flying. There were also eight individual sleeping rooms behind the main recreation room where our pilots and support crews that were on duty slept. Each room had an old rickety cot, with mosquito netting fashioned like a tent over the beds, and an old beat up school-type locker. There were no lights in the sleeping rooms so everyone maneuvered around in the dark with a flashlight. One other very important feature was the four large mouse/rat traps strategically positioned around each room. These came in handy almost every night.

One night after I had fallen asleep, I heard one of the traps go off and felt my mosquito netting dropping almost to my bed. I opened one eye and saw that a very large rat had been trapped, and the trap and the rat had fallen off the shelf onto my mosquito netting. Not wanting to get out from under the netting I just kicked the rat and the trap off the netting onto the floor. I could then hear the rat scooting around in circles on the floor as the trap did not kill the rat, it only caught him by the back legs. My initial thought was that I would get out of bed and shoot the rat with my trusty revolver. I thought better of that plan and decided I would just use my very large survival knife and stab the sucker. I got my flashlight out, found my knife and proceeded to stab the rat right to the dirt floor.

I then went back to bed and slept fairly well knowing that this rat would not bother me anymore that night. What a surprise when I woke up to daylight the next morning. The dead rat, with the knife still imbedded in his body, had been visited by other members of his pack and they had eaten almost the entire body during the night. So much for a peaceful night's sleep.

Now we did have an Air Force bomb shelter about twenty yards to the north of our hooch that we were to go into whenever the compound was under attack. It was simply a twelve-by-fifteen-by-eight-foot hole dug into the ground and covered with metal, sandbags, and an additional layer of dirt. It was located close to the hooch so we could expeditiously get to cover. The only problem was the rumors that some of the local reptiles also liked to live in the bomb shelter. The very first emergency briefing that I got when after I arrived at Quan Loi was to never enter the bomb shelter even if we were under a sustained attack. The question was would you rather be killed by an exploding rocket or by a twenty-five-foot cobra? I knew my answer, and I never did go into the bomb shelter during my entire time at Quan Loi.

We did have some defensive duties, even though we were highly paid pilots. If we were under a ground assault, we each had a pile of sandbags near the perimeter of the compound we were to go and position ourselves to take whatever defensive action we could. So, we always slept with our own personal weapons handy if we ever had to take up these defensive positions during an attack. As I said earlier, my personal weapon while at Quan Loi, besides my Smith and Wesson revolver, was an AK-47 rather than the AR-15.

Some of the Special Forces troops preferred the AK-47 if only to give them a temporary advantage over the enemy. It was thought that you could get off a few rounds from the AK-47 before the enemy knew they were being shot at. You see, the AK-47 and the AR-15 had two completely different sounds when fired. For that reason, I not only had the AK-47 for ground defense, I also carried it in my airplane with the same thought of getting off a few rounds before the enemy knew what was happening. I didn't really think through how I would parachute out of my airplane carrying an AK-47 in my arms. The other good thing about using the AK-47 was that we could have an unlimited supply of AK-47 ammunition. The U.S. ammunition for the AR-15 was closely monitored.

Whenever we needed more ammo, we just asked our Special Forces team to get us some when they were out on their next mission. The only issue with getting ammo from the enemy was the U.S. had a very special clandestine/top secret program called Eldest Son whereby U.S. troops would insert sabotaged/defective AK-47 ammo and weapons into the enemy supply chain. The ammo would be inserted by SOG teams along the enemy supply routes. The defective ammo and or weapons would explode usually killing the enemy soldier. We were very leery of getting new ammo from the field, but we pressed on and did our best with the enemy weapons and ammo.

One of the obvious questions I asked during my first night at Quan Loi was, "Where are the latrines?" I got a huge laugh out of one of my sergeants. He said, "Lieutenant, they are over by the command center about one hundred yards from the Air Force hooch. And by the way, you need to bring your own TP." So, my first trip was a real adventure. As I approached the location pointed out to me, I saw four fifty-five-gallon barrels that had been cut off about in half. They were sitting right out in the open among the rubber trees. There was a two-by-four piece of wood sitting across the barrels and that would act as the toilet seat. In order to go number two, you had to sit on the two-by-four with your butt far enough back to hit the target and then do your business. There certainly were no pretenses of privacy in these "latrines." I wonder how the female integration into our military today would handle such an arrangement. So here were our latrines. I tried very hard not to have to use the latrines at night as I am sure there were a lot of the local reptiles in the same area.

But this is not the end of the story of the latrines. On my first morning in Quan Loi after a very sleepless night as I was getting prepared to fly, I smelled the most gut-wrenching odor I have ever smelled. I asked one of our maintenance troops what that smell was. He immediately answered, "Oh, that is just the shit burners doing their job." It seemed that the sanitation protocol was for the local indigenous people that supported our compound to dispose of the waste from the day and night before. Their very sanitary approach was to pour about a gallon of aviation fuel into each barrel and light them on fire. To this day I still have that smell in my psyche.

My next burning question about Quan Loi was about food…what and where did we eat? There were a few answers to this question. If we were ever in the compound during lunch time, we could join the Special Forces for food at their chow hall. The food was OK and there were two types…the American meat and potatoes menu and then the indigenous menu of fish heads and rice. I think the meals were fifty-five cents for the U.S. troops—not a bad deal but I believe I was only on the compound for four lunch-time meals during my nine months at Quan Loi, so that wasn't the best option for me.

The second option was the famous C rations meals left over from World War II and the Korean War. We had cases and cases of those meals available. We were afraid to look at the "use by dates" as they were somewhere in the 1950's range. Now a C ration was not too bad if you were selective on the meals you choose. The C ration was an individually canned, pre-cooked, and prepared wet ration. It was intended to be issued to U.S. military land forces when fresh food or packaged unprepared food prepared in mess halls or field kitchens was not possible or not available, and when a survival ration was insufficient.

We had some choice on what C ration meals were available, but you had to be one of the first to open the case or you may end up with the dreaded Ham and Eggs choice. We called those the high explosive (HE) meals because of the incredible gas that meal would produce. Some of the better meals from the C rations were the Beef and Potatoes, Boned Turkey, Beef Steak, or Spaghetti and

Meatballs. Each C ration portion came with an accessory kit that included a chocolate bar, a can of mixed fruit, coffee and sugar packets, matches, a plastic spoon, twenty-two pieces of toilet paper, and a very ingenious tool, the P-38 can opener. The P-38 was a small, about one-and-a-half inches long, metal tool that could easily open any of the canned meals we found. Most of the troops that eat C rations in the field attached the P-38 to the chain that also held their dog tags that they wore around their neck. I also wore the P-38 around my neck but did have my dog tags muffled with two clear plastic sleeves so they would not clink together when walking.

The most amazing item in the accessory pack was a small nine-pack of filtered cigarettes. I could always find someone to trade the cigarettes for their chocolate bar. Toward the middle of my tour we were introduced to Long Range Patrol Rations, or LRPRs. LRPRs were dehydrated food packaged in a heavy plastic bag that had some fairly good options including Beef with Rice, Beef Hash, Chili Con Carne, Spaghetti and Meat Balls, Chicken Stew and Pork with Potatoes. These meals were prepared by simply pouring boiling water into the plastic bag and letting the contents warm up and rehydrate. Each meal came with an accessory pack that included a chocolate fudge bar, matches, coffee, sugar, and toilet paper. There were no cigarettes in these packages.

None of these types of field rations were like home cooking, but when you are hungry they worked just fine. They especially worked well when we had just minutes between flights and had to eat something to keep going.

I guess in an effort to make us feel like we were at home in the hot and humid jungle, a typical move by the U.S. forces was to have camp pets. We had two very friendly pet mascot dogs: Droopy and Budweiser. They were both just stray dogs that showed up around the compound one day and the Army and Air Force troops fed scraps to them from the C rations and LRRP meals.

The dogs would always stay in the Air Force hooch at night and accompany us to the flight line every time we flew. They always seemed to be waiting for us when we returned from our fights. I guess the dogs gave us a feeling of humanity in a very difficult war we were supporting. Budweiser got his name because he really liked to drink beer from his bowl, and Droopy was named for his very floppy ears. The creative lieutenants thought it would be fun if we flew Droopy with us enough times to earn an Air Medal. We only took Droopy flying if we were pretty certain we would not have an intense troops-in-contact mission. I don't know if Droopy got the required twenty mission flights for the Air Medal, but I had fun with one of our new crew chiefs on a flight with Droopy.

Droopy flew with me on a simple radio relay mission in support of one of our inserted teams. He really did not like flying but was OK most of the time unless he got airsick and threw up all over the inside if the airplane. The crew chiefs hated to have to clean up the mess after Droopy got sick in the airplane.

One day I returned from a mission flying with Droopy and taxied to the very opposite end of the runway from where we parked our airplanes. While taxing back I unstrapped and got into the right seat of the airplane and put Droopy in the left seat. Droopy put his paws on the top of the instrument panel and was looking straight ahead while I sat as low as I could in my seat. As the crew chief was marshaling me in, all he could see was Droopy's head showing in the windscreen. I never saw such a confused look on anyone's face as I saw him when he spotted Droopy "taxing" the aircraft to the parking space. In the end, there was good news for Droopy: one of our dedicated crew chiefs did all the paperwork and vaccination protocol, and he was able to take Droopy back to the States.

The news was not so good for Budweiser. As I said, the dogs always were on the flight line greeting us on our return from flight. Because the 0-2 had a front propeller that cleared the ground by only six inches, our procedure was to shut down the front engine as we taxied back to the parking ramp. The rear propeller cleared the ground by a good twenty-four inches. Well one of our new Pretzel pilots forgot to shut down the front engine and poor Budweiser was killed by the prop as he ran out to meet the aircraft. We all felt really bad for Budweiser, but one of our crew chiefs called the chow hall and asked them if they needed some additional meat for the indigenous troops in our compound as dog meat was a real delicacy in Southeast Asia.

Chapter 6
FLYING COMBAT MISSIONS IN CAMBODIA

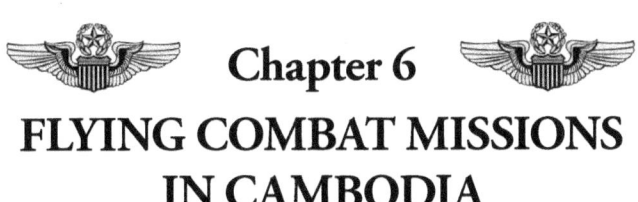

The missions I am about to describe are not because I have a photographic memory. It has been forty-eight-plus years since I flew combat in Southeast Asia. My recollections of these notable missions are based on a very detailed diary I kept on most of my missions, cross referenced with my pilot logbook and photos that I took. One of the very first tasks before I started flying combat missions in Cambodia was to get my maps up to date. This was no small task as I said before this included 181 maps that needed to be marked and catalogued.

After getting all the maps together, I began my flying missions to get to know my AOR. I started by doing a number of visual reconnaissance (VR) missions to acquaint myself with the AOR and to be able to identify landmarks. Fortunately, in the southern part of Cambodia there were major roads that crossed the country with some very large bridges that were blown up during the 1970 U.S. invasion of Cambodia. So those key landmarks were known as the first blown bridge on Highway 13 that snaked from the town of Kratie on the Mekong River to the border of South Vietnam near the town of An Loc. The second blown bridge and the third blown bridge were also on the same highway.

A couple of other significant landmarks were two prominent bends in the very wide Mekong River, the town of Kratie on the Mekong River, and the airfield at Kratie. On every single flight I tried to really observe and remember the lay of the land for future reference. Bob Johnson, my instructor for the Pretzel mission, told me that situational awareness of my AOR was the single most important skill I could bring to the mission. Since I had some experience with getting to know my AOR as an Issue FAC in South Vietnam, I completed my initial AOR familiarization with only three flights. That didn't mean I was done learning. I made it a point on each and every subsequent flight in my

AOR to note significant and insignificant landmarks, ground traffic, foot flow patterns, and other ground activity. Anything that looked different from yesterday warranted a second look.

Our mission protocol was to inform Pretzel operations of our takeoff time and general vicinity of where we would be flying on a particular mission. We would check in with Pretzel ops from time to time giving them an update on where we were in the AOR. This radio check would give a starting point, at least, if we were ever overdue on a flight and the rescue forces needed a location to start a search.

I was assigned my very first Pretzel mission on April 9. I would be leading an insert mission of six Special Force troops into an area about seventy-five kilometers east of Kratie. The insert was scheduled for April 16. These SOG missions into Cambodia had the code name Daniel Boone; the original name for the SOG missions was Prairie Fire, but that name was "leaked" by the press a few years before I arrived in SEA. Bob Johnson would be flying in my right seat monitoring the mission. However, I was the designated mission commander.

On April 9 I did the VR mission to find and locate the selected landing zone (LZ) for the insert. I was very anal in trying to remember exactly where the LZ would be in relationship to some prominent landmarks. I made a point of only flying over the LZ one time as to not give any indication to the potential enemy on the ground of where we would be operating. In addition to the primary LZ, I also designated a secondary LZ and backup LZ in case of contact with the enemy at the primary LZ.

After completing the VR mission, it was time to brief the team about the selected mission area. The briefing to the team leader was done in the SOG underground command post. Each team had a name assigned to them. Some of the teams were named for snakes, Anaconda, Cobra, or Krait, while some of the other teams had state names like California, Nevada, and Alaska. The mission briefing that I presented was very detailed with many aspects the team needed to know before the insert. This mission was a road-watching mission where the team would be inserted near a major road to watch and count the number of trucks and types of equipment that was being brought into Cambodia from the Ho Chi Min Trail complex that ran from North Vietnam through Laos into Cambodia.

The Ho Chi Min Trail was nearly 10,000 miles of a very complex system that included roads, bicycle paths, foot paths, and waterways, and initially had been a trading trail before the war. The NVA used this trail to bring supplies and troops into the war in the south.

The insert briefing included some observations about the landing zone—the best direction to go if attacked, the compass direction to the target area, the nearest back up LZ if the first one was compromised, the best escape heading if contacted by the enemy, the closest direction, and location of any population build up—and the FM ground frequency that they would be using for radio check ins and extraction if necessary. Part of this briefing was sitting at a table with the team leader and covering every detail of the map of the insert area. I would add anything that I noticed from the air that may be of interest to the planning team, for example the people that I noticed in the area, livestock trails, dense foliage, and open spaces not marked on the map.

Also at the briefing were the helicopter pilots that would be flying the team into the LZ and the Cobra gunship pilots that would be flying cover if the team got into contact with the enemy during insertion or extraction. I briefed the UHF frequency the insert helicopters would be using and the VHF radio frequency that the gunships would be using. I also described the backup LZ location if that became necessary. We briefed the rendezvous location as the first blown bridge where we would get all the aircraft together and fly as a unit to the insert site.

The preparation for each and every insert mission was extremely detailed, and the actual mission insert was usually conducted about a week after the initial briefing I presented to the team. The team leader, known as One Zero, would prepare and brief his team on every single aspect of the mission from the terrain and the target to the intelligence for that area and the equipment they would utilize on the mission. The team would then practice each step of the process. They would test all of the equipment they would take with them on the mission and "muffled" every piece of gear they would take into the field with tape or rubber bands so they generated no rattle, clank, or noise of any kind.

One unique disguise technique the SOG teams would sometimes use was to wear NVA uniforms that would really confuse the enemy in the initial phase of an encounter. That technique was also a challenge when the FAC directed the recovery of a team from a landing zone and saw six to eight troops wearing NVA uniforms being prepared to be extracted. The SOG teams used mostly foreign weapons that were untraceable.

The insert plan would be that I would take off about thirty to forty-five minutes before the scheduled insert time and do a weather check to make sure the mission was a go. On the morning of April 16, the cloud cover was broken at about 3,500 feet. The visibility was good, and I made the call as the mission commander to launch the four helicopters. I made a point of flying nowhere near the LZ.

In some cases, we would pick out a fictional target about five to ten kilometers from the selected LZ and shoot a couple of WP rockets in the ground. We thought maybe this would give the enemy an idea that we were attacking a different location and they would not be observant of the actual LZ activity. Once the helicopters were airborne, I made a radio check with them and proceeded to the first blown bridge for our rendezvous. The helicopters were at about 1,500 feet and I was at 2,000 feet. We all had a good visual contact with each other and proceeded to the LZ.

Once we were near the LZ I told the lead insert helicopter that I would visually mark the LZ. Our procedure was to fly to below treetop level and once over the LZ call out "Bingo, Bingo, Bingo." This would indicate to the insert helicopter that this was the proper LZ. The gunship helicopters would position themselves to be able to immediately put fire on either side of the LZ if there was enemy contact during the insert. The insert helicopter said he had a good visual on the LZ and was proceeding with the insert. The insert helicopter landed safely in the LZ, and I saw the team depart the helicopter and head east into the thick jungle cover.

Fortunately, on this mission there was no enemy response to the insert and the helicopters departed to the south to return to Quan Loi. The insert protocol required the insert FAC to remain airborne until we got our first radio check-in from the team on the predetermined FM frequency… normally that first check-in took place thirty minutes to one hour after insert. The radio contact FAC would orbit at about 3,500 feet, well away from the team but still within line of site for a radio check. On this mission the team leader called with a radio check at about the forty-five-minute point and told me they were in position and safe. I confirmed that we would get a next radio and condition check at about 1800 hours later that day.

Normal procedure would be a radio check at 0600 and 1800 each day until the team had completed their mission. Many a mission would be terminated sooner if the team came in direct contact with the enemy or the mission was completed successfully before the scheduled extract time. This mission went just as planned, and I was now certified to run future missions on my own. However, not all the future inserts I supported went as smoothly as this one.

High Low Missions: Another aspect of our unique FAC support to the SOG mission was the crazy High Low missions that we flew along with the 5th Special Forces Aviation Battalion and other SOG personnel. Since there were few actual reconnaissance assets available to fly photo reconnaissance missions in Cambodia, the SOG team came up with a plan where we could fly our own organic photo reconnaissance missions. These missions involved the use of an Army 0-1 Bird Dog flying at tree top level with an enlisted SOG combat photographer in the back seat taking pictures of anything that looked like a war target. An 0-2 FAC would fly about 500 to 1,000 feet above and behind the O-1 with a map spread out in his lap numbering each mark on a 1:50,000 map that the photographer called out.

Following the flight, the photos were developed and matched up with the corresponding numbers on the FACs map. In this way we could match an exact location of any interesting equipment or activity to a precise geographical location. Unbeknown to the FAC squadron, which by now was the 21 TASS located at Phan Rang in South Vietnam, the Pretzel FACs carried defensive rockets on these High Low missions. The rockets were seventeen-pound high explosive (HE) or flechette rockets and were to be used in an emergency if the low bird on a High Low mission was taking fire and needed to exit the area in a hurry. I preferred to carry one pod of the HE and one pod of the flechette rockets because that would give me seven rockets in each pod and the rockets were carried on opposite wings. During the time I was at Quan Loi I flew forty-two High Low missions and every one of them brought a great deal of excitement.

One specific High Low mission on July 14 really tested my skill and cunning. We were tasked to take photos along the Mekong River near the town of Kratie. We had known for quite some time that Kratie was being used by the NVA and the VC as a storage center for a lot of their supplies. We later found out that the supply build-up in and around Kratie was for the NVA invasions of South Vietnam in 1972 and 1975.

We were determined to find out how they were getting their supplies into Kratie. I took off at 0400 and flew down to Saigon to pick up the enlisted photographer, a Marine gunnery sergeant, and returned to Quan Loi just at dawn to brief with the 0-1 pilot. Our plan was to be on the river in the early morning hours and take photos of any activity that could indicate how those supplies were getting into Kratie.

Fortunately, the weather was very good with no low-level clouds so we would have a very good opportunity to get some quality photos if anything was taking place. The 0-1 flew very low, almost at water level, right along the bank of the river. We were going to fly from south to north and pass the main part of Kratie at about thirty minutes into the low-level flight. I was positioned above and behind the 0-1 at about 1,000 feet. I had to do a bit of maneuvering to keep the sun to my side as the sun was rapidly rising in the east. I also needed to keep the 0-1 in sight at all times and have my maps readily available to annotate each mark that was called out. I had done enough of these High Low missions that I knew I needed to have my maps prepositioned and sequenced for easy access as we flew the reconnaissance route along the river. We were about twenty minutes into the low-level portion when all hell broke loose.

Just as we passed a small tributary river that flowed into the Mekong the low bird called out that he was taking small arms fire just north of the tributary. I had already armed both wing rocket pods before we descended for the mission and immediately fired off two flechette rockets into an area I guessed the ground fire was coming from. I could not see the actual shooters, but my goal was to at least get the bad guys to stop shooting so the 0-1 could immediately escape. I saw the 0-1 make a very hard left turn over the river and I believe I saw water splashing as he tried to get away from the ground fire. At this point I could see about ten soldiers shooting at the 0-1, and I then shot off four of my high-explosive rockets from the left-wing pod. Now when a 2.75-inch folding fin rocket is shot it gets to supersonic speed before it hits the ground. The sound of the incoming rocket is usually enough to get the bad guys to keep their heads down. In this case the bad guys just kept shooting at the 0-1 and then at my aircraft. In a last desperate attempt to get us out of there safely I salvoed all my remaining rockets into where the fire was coming from.

I watched as the 0-1 completed his left turn over the river and was now flying southwest back toward the opposite riverbank and away from the ground fire. I made a very hard climbing right turn and also headed away from the riverbank area. Finally the shooting stopped, and I picked up sight of the 0-1 climbing back to altitude.

We both climbed to about 1,500 feet, and I joined in close formation with the 0-1 so that we could check each aircraft for any battle damage. It was very obvious that the 0-1 had taken a few hits. Most of the damage I saw was on the rear part of the fuselage behind the cockpit area. The 0-1 pilot said his engine was running fine and that he was headed back to Quan Loi.

He said he did not see any obvious damage to my aircraft, and I followed him back to Quan Loi for a safe landing. Once on the ground we both inspected our aircraft; the 0-1 had seventeen small-arms holes in the aircraft. My 0-2 had three small-arms holes in the right tail boom. Taking hits in our aircraft earned us the nickname of magnet asses!

The photo analysis of this mission showed that the NVA or VC were using the tributary of the Mekong River to move their supplies into the Kratie area. They would then transport the supplies up the Mekong. We caught them just as they were entering the Mekong and that is probably why we had such a fierce reaction to our overflight of those operations. I don't believe we ever got approval to strike the massive amount of supplies we could see right out in the open in Kratie. How frustrating to put our service members at risk finding solid intelligence material and then not acting on the info. But that was the way our war was fought on an almost daily basis.

Chapter 7
CONDUCTING AN AIR STRIKE

As I mentioned before there were two types of air strikes: preplanned and immediate. The best way to describe these air strikes is to relate one strike mission that I supported on July 30, 1971. This mission was an immediate airstrike as one of our inserted teams had made contact with a fairly large enemy force. They had been sent to observe another potential storage site of enemy supplies and were in the field only two days when they encountered a large contingent of NVA/VC forces. The insert, done two days earlier, had gone smoothly and all the radio calls were non-eventful until the team gave an emergency update at the 1800 check-in on July 30.

The team radioed that they had spotted the storage site but had also been detected by the enemy forces near the storage site. They were heading to the emergency landing zone that had been briefed prior to the start of the mission. I immediately called a Prairie Fire Emergency, which signified that a team was in trouble and needed immediate air support and extract. I quickly contacted Ramrod Control, the airborne command and control C-130 aircraft, and asked for any air support available to assist in the Prairie Fire Emergency.

Simultaneously I called back to Pretzel Ops and requested the extract team and four Cobra Gunships be put on strip alert, meaning they would be ready to launch on my request. As it was getting toward the end of the day and sunset, I wanted to get the fighters on target as soon as possible. Ramrod informed me they had diverted two A-37s, Rap 21 and Rap 22, and would rendezvous with me in about twelve minutes. The very first thing I had to do was sort out where our team was located, the direction of travel they were taking to get to the LZ, and where the enemy forces were located. This contact was done on a dedicated FM radio. I could tell the enemy was fairly close as I could hear the anxiety in the team leader's voice. Since I could see that the team was less than one kilometer from the LZ, I advised Quan Loi to launch the strip alert birds, Kingbee 33 and 34, and four Cobra Gunships, call signs Raider 21, 22, 23 and 24. They would have about a twenty-minute flight to the LZ.

I had finally spotted the enemy troops that were about 300 meters behind the team and looked like they were closing fast. It seemed to me like there were about thirty of them. Just then Rap flight advised me that they had visual contact with me and would orbit at 10,000 feet. They had about thirty minutes of fuel remaining, and each had three 500-pound MK-82 bombs and three CBU-24 cluster bombs, in addition to several hundred rounds of 7.62 ammo mounted in a nose gun. Before any air strike took place the FAC would brief the fighters on the parameters of the mission. Some of the material briefed by the FAC to the fighters included:

Target description
Target location
Desired results
Target elevation
Location of friendlies
Landmarks
Run in heading
Break heading
Bailout direction
Observed weather
Enemy location
Ground fire expected
Location of guns
FAC location
Desired sequence of bombs
No bomb Line

Once all the briefing material was covered and the fighters acknowledged they understood, it was time for the show to begin. I would call "FAC in for the mark," meaning that I would attempt to place a WP rocket exactly where I wanted the first bomb to hit. If the rocket and I performed as desired, I would clear the first fighter in with a call, "hit my smoke," meaning drop the first bomb on my smoke. Most of the time, the intention was to drop the first bomb fifty meters or so to the north or south of my smoke. It was not necessary to hit the target with the WP, only to give the fighters a reference on which to set up their aim point for ordnance delivery. I would then call "cleared hot," which meant the first fighter could proceed with the attack and that I had cleared the fighter to expend their ordnance. On this first pass I requested the MK-82 500-pound bombs. I felt that the large explosion from those bombs would force the enemy to keep their heads down.

As soon as I saw the first bomb hit the ground, I would adjust the second fighter to hit either on the same spot as the lead or about fifty meters to the north of the lead fighter's bomb. During this mission both fighters hit exactly where I needed them to hit. During the first A-37 run in there was a large number of small arms rounds fired at the fighters and at my aircraft. Fortunately, none of the rounds hit any aircraft. I checked with my team on the ground to make sure the bombs were not too close to them. In this case my ground team said the shooting from the bad guys had subsided a bit and they were nearly at the backup LZ. Just as that call was confirmed the extract team made radio contact with me and said they were five minutes out.

I called the fighters and told them to make the second pass in the same direction and drop on the same location. I cleared flight lead in with another "cleared hot" call. After I saw the second bomb from the flight lead, I told number two to drop in the same location and after dropping to hold for the insert of the extract helicopters. I wanted the fighters to drop their last 500-pound bombs about one hundred meters to the southeast of their first two bombs and then follow up with CBU—a cluster bomb unit—while the extract was taking place. The CBUs were carried in a canister fixed to an external mount under the wing of a fighter. Each CBU canister carried hundreds of small bomblets about the size of a baseball. Each bomblet was filled with hundreds of 3/8 inch steel ball bearings and employed varying fusing options from impact to delayed detonation. There were no small arms fired during the second A-37 pass.

Fortunately, there was a very prominent dry creek bed between their first bomb drop location and the LZ. I directed no bombs southeast of the creek bed. We called this a bomb line and that gave the fighters a solid visual reference to not drop any munitions on a designated side of the line. In this case the dry creek bed was the bomb line. I then got a call from the extract helicopters and the Cobra Gunships that they had me and the A-37s in sight. I immediately contacted the team on the ground and told them to proceed to the backup LZ and be ready for pick up in three minutes.

I briefed the extract helicopters and the gunships on the VHF and UHF channels of my plan. I wanted the backup extract helicopter to orbit at 1,500 feet southeast of the LZ while the primary extract helicopter landed in the LZ and picked up the team. I directed the Cobras to fly escort on either side the extract helicopter and strafe both sides of the LZ as the extract chopper landed in the LZ.

Simultaneously on the UHF channel, I cleared the A-37's to drop their final 500-pound bombs on their previous target and then follow up with two CBU's in the same general area. Since the A-37s target was 500 meters northwest of the LZ, I cleared them in hot for their bomb and CBU drops. That part of the plan worked perfectly, and I am sure the enemy was hunkered down and or killed in the subsequent drops. I then descended to tree top level to mark the LZ with the standard "Bingo, Bingo, Bingo" call. The lead helicopter acknowledged that he had the LZ in site and was prepared to land and pick up the team. The extraction went as planned with no ground fire noted. We extracted the team just as official sunset was over the LZ.

Before the A-37s and the extract helicopters departed the area, I requested the four Cobras remain on station while I did a bomb damage assessment on the bomb and CBU drops. For the BDA, the FAC would brief the fighters on how effective their munition drops were. We would tell them how long they were on target, the percentage of munitions on target, and the damage that they caused. If observed, we always added a body count of enemy killed in action (KIA) or wounded in action (WIA).

On this particular BDA I spotted about sixteen NVA/VC bodies near the bomb craters from the 500-pound bombs. Also saw two more bodies near the CBU drop. I passed the BDA on to the A-37s as all bombs on target, eighteen enemy troops KIA and unknown number of WIA. I also relayed that the team was successfully extracted and thanked them for a job well done. This was just a standard day in the life of a Pretzel FAC.

Cessna C-150

Cessna C-172 (T-41)

Cessna T-37

Northrop T-38

Lockheed AT-33

Cessna O-2A

Chris Hudnot and Tom

Ed Hooker and Tom

Pretzel/Rash FAC Hootch, Bien Hoa

Pretzel/Rash FAC Hootch, Bien Hoa

19th TASS Building, Bien Hoa

Crashed O-2, Bien Hoa

Quan Loi, Looking Toward the SE

Quan Loi Runway

Inside Quan Loi Compound

Mammasan, Quan Loi Compound

Pretzel Hootch, Quan Loi

Inside Pretzel Hootch, Quan Loi

Snake Infested Bomb Shelter, Quan Loi

Sapper Attack, Quan Loi

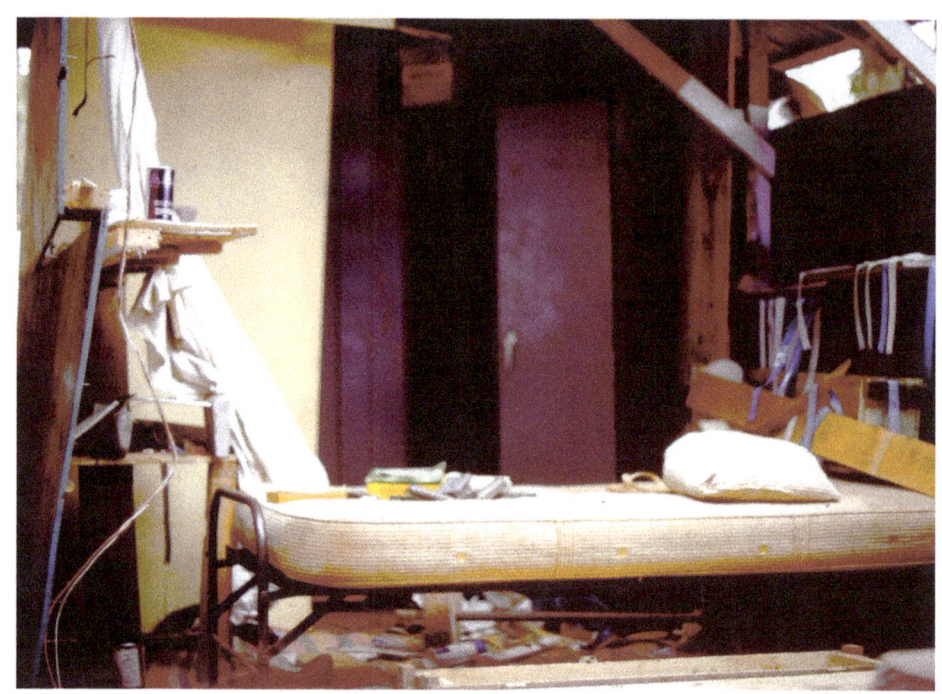

Inside Sapper Attack, Quan Loi

Budweiser and Droopy, Quan Loi

Quan Loi Mansion

Quan Loi Swimming Pool

Command Vault

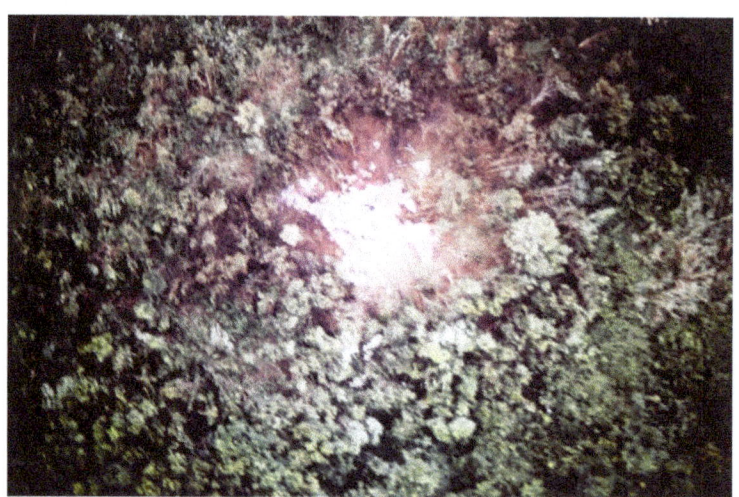

Newendorp RF-4 Crash Site

Moving Supplies to the Mekong River

Kratie Prison

Chapter 7

Supply Depot, Kratie, Cambodia

Sampan of Supplies, Mekong River

Buddhist Temple, Kratie, Cambodia

Angor Wat, Cambodia

Angor Wat, Cambodia

Ban Me Thuot, South Vietnam

Cerano the FAC Monkey, Ban Me Thuot

FAC Memorial, Colorado Springs

FAC Memorial, Colorado Springs

Misty FAC Memorial, Colorado Springs

Misty FAC Memorial, Colorado Springs

JTAC Memorial, Colorado Springs

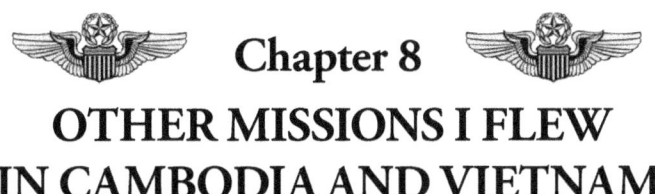

Chapter 8
OTHER MISSIONS I FLEW IN CAMBODIA AND VIETNAM

Visual Reconnaissance: One of the most basic and probably most critical missions that all FACs accomplished was the Visual Reconnaissance flight. We could be expected to perform this mission on every single flight we took. Our task was to be hyper-observant of everything that we could see in our Area of Responsibility (AOR). Visual reconnaissance formed the core FAC mission during the war as we flew as low and slow as safety, or squadron regulations, would allow us to maintain constant aerial surveillance. As I mentioned before, each FAC was assigned to a specific AOR.

Our task was to notice any changes that may have occurred since a previous flight. That meant that as we flew over a river crossing, we took notice of signs of either foot traffic or vehicle traffic that wasn't there the last time we flew over that area. We would look for different color foliage that may have changed from a previous flight. We could also tell if there were more people working in the fields than we saw on an earlier flight. We took note of the clothing the people wore in the villages or working in the fields, misplaced vegetable patches, the absence of water buffalo, or smoke from cooking fires in the jungles. We could also tell if the buildup of supplies had increased from one flight to the next. All of these changes in signs could indicate that enemy forces were in the area. All the while, we would have to transfer the information we collected to one of our numerous maps so we could pass that to the intelligence folks for future action.

Radio Relay Mission: One key mission I flew was the radio relay mission in support of our inserted Special Forces teams. After we inserted a team, we had two daily prescheduled radio check-in times with each team. We would attempt to make radio contact at 0600 in the morning and 1800 in the evening every day the team was in the field. For the most part these radio checks were all routine, unless they weren't. We never knew during our radio checks if the team was in peril and needed an immediate extract. If that situation came about, the SOG folks at Ban Me Thot or Quan Loi really had to scramble to put a rescue team in place for an extraction. On July 10 I flew my longest single mission: 5.6 hours of flight time on a radio replay mission as I had trouble finding and then making contact with the inserted team.

We always took off with full fuel tanks just in case we had to stick around and control the extract forces. Toward the end of my time as a Pretzel and Mike FAC we started to support completely indigenous Special Forces teams. We obviously had a language issue trying to talk to the indigenous teams on the ground. The solution was to fly an interpreter with us on the radio relay missions.

Our interpreters were usually multi-language "capable" South Vietnamese lieutenants. For the most part they were good troops but were very uncomfortable flying. The interpreter vomited on almost every flight he took with me. What a mess, although we had no choice but to keep on flying our radio relay mission. I had one very critical mission with an interpreter that almost ended in disaster.

On this particular flight I took a large barrage of small arms ground fire; the front engine of the 0-2 was hit and put out of commission. I was not sure if I could safely keep the aircraft airborne to return to Quan Loi. As I discussed the possibility of us having to bail out of the airplane, the Vietnamese lieutenant in the right seat froze with fear and was not responding to me or my briefing on the possibility of bailing out of the airplane. Now in the 0-2 the only way to bail out of the aircraft was through the right door. The problem was that I had a frozen lieutenant in the right seat. I ran through some of my options if the bailout became necessary.

As I turned the airplane back toward Quan Loi, I was not certain I could make it back with full fuel (I had already jettisoned my fourteen rockets) and had an extra passenger in the airplane. My plan was very straight forward: I would pull out my trusty .38 caliber revolver, shoot the lieutenant, open the door, push the body out of the airplane, and parachute to safety. I had my hand on the gun when I realized I might just be able to get back to base. Thankfully I made it to a safe landing. Following the landing I demanded that this lieutenant never fly with us again. As far as I know that was the end of his interpreter flying days.

Arc Light Bomb Damage Assessment (BDA): One of the most interesting and challenging missions that I also flew as a Pretzel FAC was bomb damage assessments (BDA) for the B-52 Bomber Arc Light missions. The real tactical value of these bombing missions was suspect, but I believe the strategic and psychological value was superb. Arc Light was the code name for the overwhelming aerial raids of the

B-52 Stratofortress bombers against enemy positions in Southeast Asia. Initially the B-52s were stationed at Anderson Air Force Base in Guam, but later in the war some were also staged out of U-Tapao, Thailand.

The B-52 Arc Light missions were conducted from above 30,000 feet so the enemy never knew what hit them as the bombs started impacting. The B-52s usually flew three to a bombing cell and their bombs were dropped in an overlapping pattern. The B-52s assigned to the Arc Light missions were involved in several types of operations: air interdiction, strategic bombing, and, in some very rare occasions, close air support. The B-52s that I did BDA for were B-52Ds and would carry 108 conventional bombs: eighty-four MK 82 500-pound bombs internally and twenty-four MK 84 750-pound bombs on the wing pylons.

Most of the time the targets for the Arc Light missions came from higher headquarters; however, sometimes when we found a very lucrative target on one of our High Low missions we requested Arc Light support through our SOG headquarters. For the Arc Light BDA missions this was always a preplanned mission and designated with the standard six-digit map coordinates. Once we were briefed on the actual drop point, we would fly to an area some three kilometers from the initial drop point and orbit waiting for the first bombs. I was very uneasy on these missions so I always tripled checked the map coordinates to make sure I was not "shot down" by a bomb from a B-52.

The U.S. command in Saigon did the most amazingly stupid thing in support of these Arc Light missions: just before the drop, approximately thirty minutes prior to the first bomb drop, the U.S. military would announce a warning over the Guard Frequency (243.0 MHz) to prevent aircraft from wandering into the bombing area. U.S. pilots could plot the impact point within a mile or so and guess what…so could the enemy. Most of the time we could see the contrails of the bombers making their pass and we would be ready to drop down to about 500 feet to make a low pass along the bomb destruction line.

Our job was to report any consequential damage and report back to the SOG headquarters. However, on most BDA runs all we saw was jungle destruction as the bombs did a great job of tearing up the land. The craters from the 750-pound bombs were about twelve feet deep and fifteen feet wide.

On one BDA run I did see something very strange: a white Ford pickup that was lying on its side with three individuals in various poses on the ground certainly dead from the impacts of the bombs. There was a fairly well-prepared dirt and gravel road that ran perpendicular to the B-52 bombing run and, unfortunately for the enemy, they crossed right through the bomb pattern. What a bad-luck day for those three individuals…timing is everything in war. Occasionally we would also find a supply bunker or building completely destroyed. I was always concerned about potential secondary explosions.

Commando Vault: Another very unique mission I flew as an Issue FAC was supporting a mission called Commando Vault. This unique mission involved a C-130 cargo aircraft dropping a 15,000-pound bomb out of the back of the aircraft primarily to clear a landing zone for future operations. The bomb was attached to a set of parachutes: one parachute to pull the pallet holding the BLU-82 bomb out of the aircraft and then another parachute attached to the bomb to let it fall to the ground. The bomb had a three-foot fuse extender, called a daisy cutter, attached to the nose of the bomb that would make sure the bomb exploded above the ground and not dig a crater in the ground.

The theory was that if you dropped the bomb in a very heavily forested jungle the blast and explosion from the expanding trees would clear an area sufficient to land two helicopters for the insertion of combat ground teams. The BLU-82 used a fuel-air explosive (FAE) consisting only of an agent and a dispersing mechanism and would take its oxidizers from the oxygen in the air. The BLU-82 system depended upon the accurate positioning of the aircraft by either a fixed ground radar or on-board navigation equipment. The ground radar controller, or aircrew navigator if applicable, was responsible for positioning the aircraft prior to final countdown and release.

The FAC's role in this mission was to find the appropriate location to drop the bomb. Consideration of that location was proximity to the objective of the later ground forces team and the density of the jungle where the bomb was dropped. We would get briefed on the final objective location of the upcoming mission and it was our job to do visual reconnaissance to determine the location to drop. Once again, very precise map reading was absolutely essential for the success of the mission. If the jungle was not thick enough for the blast effect or if the desired ground objective was too far from the blast site, we had to evaluate and determine the closest area that would work for the insert. The information that we would pass back to the Army unit was the eight-digit map coordinates where the bomb should be dropped.

One such mission I supported was on March 31, 1971. Following the Cambodia invasion in 1970 we had noticed a lot of truck traffic near the border of Cambodia and South Vietnam and felt that there was a staging area just inside the Cambodian side of the border. There was no suitable LZ near the staging area, so a Commando Vault mission was deemed necessary. I flew a VR mission in that vicinity on March 26 to find a suitable location. The location I selected was about two kilometers from the suspected activity. The future LZ had very dense jungle foliage, and I thought it would be a good location to do the insert. The coordinates were passed through the 25th Infantry Division channels to the Air Force, and the Commando Vault mission and the follow-on LZ insert were scheduled.

Since I was the FAC that designated the drop location, I was scheduled to fly and observe the drop. I established an orbit about two kilometers to the south of the drop location, not wanting to be north flying near the suspected storage area. I had visual contact of the C-130 flying in for his drop. He was at about 10,000 feet as the blast pattern or safe zone of a BLU-82 drop could be up to 7,000 feet. I did not see the bomb come out of the aircraft but did see the parachute once the bomb separated from the pallet. In no time it looked like a nuclear bomb had been dropped in the jungle. The mushroom-shaped dust cloud easily went up to about 6,000 feet, and I waited for the debris to stop falling before I flew a BDA pattern over the drop site.

Dropping down to about 500 feet, I could see that the BLU-82 had done its job and two Huey helicopters could easily use the new LZ to insert the recon team. The only issue I noted was that some of the tree stumps away from the center of the blast area were still about one to two feet tall. There should be no problem if the helicopters did a hover off load. I called back to the 25th ops and told them that the LZ was cleared and they could launch the insert helicopters.

As I waited for contact with the insert helicopters, I got a call on my UHF (KY-28) secure radio that the insert mission had been aborted due to some political issues with clearance from the South Vietnamese officials. Many times, the clearance for a very timely mission was not received by our U.S. officials because the South Vietnamese coordinator, usually the Province Chief, would not give approval for the mission. Being just a lieutenant, the decision was well beyond my pay grade, and I accepted the abort. At least we made a few more million jungle toothpicks with the BLU-82 drop.

Combat Search and Rescue (CSAR): Combat Search and Rescue Missions (CSAR) were one of the most challenging, frustrating, and rewarding missions I flew. During my twelve months in combat I flew six of these CSAR missions. The role of the FAC in any CSAR mission was to act as the On-Scene Tactical Commander of the entire rescue operation. When I say tactical, I mean we managed and directed all the resources that we had requested and had been approved by the in-country CSAR resource center. Many factors went into a

CSAR mission, including the location of the downed pilot, the condition of the downed pilot (if we knew the condition), the terrain, the enemy in the area, the firepower of the enemy, the weather, the time of day (night rescues were nearly impossible), and, finally, the type of CSAR resources sent to us and their ability.

During my time in Southeast Asia the resources in support of a CSAR mission were varied based on the availability of resources and the distance to the CSAR location. In a perfect CSAR scenario those resources would include two HH-53 Helicopters, call sign Jolley Green Giant, and two to four A1-E Douglas fighters, usually with a Sandy call sign. The A-1E was a very sturdy WWII propeller-driven fighter that had a very long loiter time and a wide array of weapons to protect both the aviator on the ground and the rescue helicopters. Also, on-board the rescue helicopters were the very brave pararescue men known as PJs. The PJ's mission was to descend into the jungle on a mechanical hoist and stabilize the shot-down pilot and help him into the rescue hoist. While the HH-53's and the A-1Es were the desired CSAR package, we would use any helicopter, fighters, or attack helicopters available to conduct a successful CSAR.

Normally if an airman had been shot down there were fierce enemy forces in the immediate area. The only exception to this was if the downed airman had been able to egress the hot area and fly to a safer ejection/bailout out point. Many times, the best option was to fly to a "feet wet" position over the South China Sea and hope for a naval ship or helicopter pick up. Unfortunately, all the CASR missions I flew were over contested enemy territory. The CSAR missions I participated in involved U.S. and Vietnamese fighter aircraft and helicopters.

One particular CSAR mission on October 1, 1971, was the most memorable of my 535 combat sorties that I flew in Southeast Asia. I must explain the 535 number. The Air Force, in 1971, had a very unique way of counting combat missions for FACs. For counting purposes, the FACs combat mission would only be counted as one combat mission per calendar day no matter how many actual missions or sorties you flew on that day. So according to Air Force records I flew combat missions for only 237 different days. According to my official Air Force Flight Records and my personal flight log, my total combat flying time was 752.7 hours over the 535 combat sorties, not combat mission days. October 1, 1971, started out as just another normal day of flying in Southeast Asia.

Following yet another morning High Low mission I had a LRRP for lunch. I was scheduled to fly what I called a fairly boring mission that afternoon…a visual reconnaissance mission looking for a landing zone in Cambodia to insert a Special Forces team. This mission was preceded by an intelligence briefing about the specific mission the team would perform; this future mission was another road-watching mission. I needed to fly an offset pattern and determine the terrain, possible emergency extract landing zones, and any other information that might help the team succeed and survive the three to seven days of their mission. My biggest fear was that I couldn't find the LZ that I briefed and put the team in the wrong location.

I was flying just across the Cambodian border and as the afternoon thunderstorms came rolling in, I heard an emergency locator beacon, called a beeper, signaling that an aircraft had gone down. The beeper was a UHF transmitter attached to an aircrew's parachute. Upon separating from the ejection seat, a lanyard would automatically activate the beeper and provide a UHF homing signal to the downed aviator. The beeper would be used by rescue forces to find the downed aviator. A beeper could be turned off manually by the downed aviator since the beeper would jam all other emergency communications on the Guard Frequency (243.0 MHz). Unfortunately, the beeper could also be used by the enemy to locate the downed aviator.

I scanned the horizon and saw the column of black smoke rising in the air. I was over the crash site in less than five minutes and arrived on scene at approximately 1410. An OV-10 FAC, Rustic 14, and an airborne Command Post, King 25, were already on scene. They were in contact with a Falcon 33B on the ground. At approximately 1415, Rustic 14 passed on-scene command to me as he was low on fuel and needed to return to base. King 25 notified me that two Jolley Green HH-53 helicopters were airborne but were about fifty minutes out. Knowing that such a delay could impact a successful recovery, I called back to our Special Forces base at Quan Loi and requested any helicopter available to launch for the recovery. Quan Loi said they would launch two H-34 King Bee Vietnamese helicopters for the rescue. H-34 helicopters were mid-1950's vintage U.S. helicopters and were flown by the 219th South Vietnamese Air Force Squadron that had four aircraft on alert at all times to support the SOG mission.

Quan Loi operations also said that an Army 0-1, Aloft 54, would lead the helicopters to the crash site. Since the crash site was only approximately fifteen miles from Quan Loi, I knew they could arrive on scene well before the rescue HH-53s. I did get good radio and visual contact with the back seater of the downed aircraft, Falcon 33B. I determined that if the survivor was in OK condition and was mobile, he could move to a suitable pick up spot if required. I knew it was the back seater of a two-seat aircraft because at that time the call signs of two-seat fighter aircraft designated the front seater as Alpha and the back seater as Bravo. Hence Falcon 33B, the Weapons Systems Operator (WSO), was the back seater and the front seater would be Falcon 33A, the pilot of the aircraft. However, there was still no radio contact with the front seat pilot. The afternoon weather had started to deteriorate and there were ceilings as low as 500 feet in the immediate rescue area. Fortunately, there was very minimal small-arms ground fire in the rescue area, and it did not pose a direct problem to the rescue attempt.

Based on the terrain, I knew that Falcon 33B could not be picked up from his present location because of the dense jungle he was in. The Vietnamese helicopters did not have the sophisticated jungle penetrator equipment on board to pull a survivor from the thick underbrush. I did find a suitable landing zone for the H-34 about one hundred meters to the northwest of Falcon 33B's current location. While the helicopters were still in bound, I had Falcon 33B start his movement to the LZ. After no more than fifteen minutes a King Bee helicopter landed in the LZ and picked up the downed WSO.

I remained on scene to coordinate any effort to locate the front seat pilot who was still not in contact with me. About thirty minutes later the HH-53 Helicopters arrived and had two PJs on board. The PJ's exited the helicopter and proceeded to the crash site. After a very short time on the ground the PJ team informed me that they found the remains of the front seat pilot still in the cockpit. They said they would remove the pilot and fly him back to our base at Quan Loi. The Air Force also decided that it was too dangerous to leave any potential classified material at the crash site, so the PJs were ordered to use explosives to destroy the remaining cockpit area of the crashed RF-4 aircraft.

As I said before, Quan Loi was a very remote site with no medical support or refrigeration to store the body until the next day. By the time I returned to the base, the two HH-53 helicopters had departed and were enroute back to their staging base at Bahn Me Thuot. I tried to convince a Vietnamese helicopter crew that was on alert at Quan Loi to fly the remains back to our main base at Tan Son Nhut. They refused because the weather was too bad to fly. So, I loaded the body (it was in a body bag) on the back seat of my aircraft and I flew it back to the main base. There was no way I would allow the body to stay the night at Quan Loi. Boy, I should have listened to the helicopter pilots. But what the heck, I was a lieutenant—what was the worst thing the Air Force could do to me…send me to Southeast Asia as a FAC?

By the time I took off I still had about forty-five minutes left before sunset. I had barely got the gear up when I got a call from our ops that we had a TIC, or troops in contact, a Prairie Fire Emergency, and I needed to head to their location, about twenty-five miles inside Cambodia. You can imagine how loud the "F" word came out of my mouth. A TIC meant that the team we had inserted a few days earlier was now in a direct firefight with the enemy. The enemy contact was most likely NVA forces, as we had observed large numbers of them infiltrating the trails in Laos and Cambodia during the previous few months. The weather was marginal at best, about a 400-foot ceiling (but during a TIC all the normal flight restrictions were waived), and I pressed on and made radio contact with the team. I then coordinated and controlled an extract mission with a pair of Air Force UH-1N Green Hornet helicopters, Green Hornet 23 and 24, that were on strip alert at another SF base called Ban Me Thuot, and two Army Cobra gunships, Raider 31 and 32, from Quan Loi. Due to the low ceiling, I knew I would not be able to use any fighters on this extract.

While maneuvering for the extract, I realized that I had not strapped the body bag to the back seat of my aircraft, and the body bag almost flew over the front seat and joined me in the cockpit a few times. It was quite a show with me trying to fly, talk to the team on the ground on FM radio, the Cobra Gunships on VHF radio and the Green Hornets on UHF radio, and keep the body bag in place on the back seat. The smell of burned flesh filled the cockpit, and I thought I was going to puke a few times. It was just like seeing a monkey trying to screw a football. I finally located the team, moved them to an LZ, prepped the LZ with fire from the Cobras, and safely extracted them. The helicopters that extracted the team were able to fly back to Loc Ninh, a fire support base about five miles west of Quan Loi, as our little base was completely socked in by the weather.

By the time the extract was completed and I headed south to Tan Son Nhut, it was dark and the weather was really bad.... very severe thunderstorms, rain, and lightning everywhere. I was out of ideas, had no place to divert to and had few options. The thunderstorms were so widespread I could not fly around them or over them in my light aircraft...I had to press on right through the storm line. While the trip was only about one hundred miles from my location in Cambodia to Tan Son Nhut, it was probably one of the most harrowing flights I had of my 503 combat missions in Southeast Asia I knew that I would not get shot down on this flight as the weather was so bad that even the North Vietnamese Army and Viet Cong gunners were taking shelter. The severe turbulence from the thunderstorms threw the aircraft around violently, then lightning struck the left-wing tip of my aircraft, flowed right through the aircraft, across my body, and exited out the right wing-tip light. I found the damage to the wing tip after I landed.

Because of a design flaw in the O-2, rainwater was pouring in the top of the wind screen, soaking me and all the instruments in the aircraft. I was convinced that the aircraft would disintegrate before I landed. My only thought was that I had a mission to get that body back to the main base, how would it look if

I crashed with the body that was in my care? I used all the instrument flying skills that I had in my short flying career to keep my aircraft in flight and avoid spatial disorientation. I kept remembering my T-37 instructor pilot from Reese Air Force Base telling me "cross check, cross check, cross check." My thoughts were of the crash rescue crew that would examine the wreckage of my aircraft and try to figure out how the hell the pilot got into the body bag before the crash.

I had done a lot of praying on other hairy missions but this time my prayers were very direct to God…please get me through this crisis and I will be a much better person, I will never miss church again, I will read the Bible every day, I will pray three times a day, I won't tell another dirty joke, I won't drink as much, and anything else I could think of. I was sure hoping that God remembered me since I had not been a real good prayer partner with God up until that time. I guess I was negotiating with God. Thanks goodness He heard my prayers. While still inbound I had the base tower contact the Army morgue and request that they meet my aircraft after I landed. After the most terrifying forty-five minutes of my entire flying career, I completed an instrument approach into Tan Son Nhut and landed safely. It was raining so hard when I landed that I needed a "follow me truck" to guide me to the parking spot.

When the ambulance met my aircraft, I am not sure if they thought maybe I was the casualty as I was soaking wet, white as a sheet, and very uneasy on my feet. But after some very direct discussion with the ambulance crew they realized that the body bag was on the back seat of the aircraft. I was relieved that I had landed safely and wanted nothing more than to get to the club as fast as I could for a few beers. The Army folks said, "Not so fast lieutenant. You have to go to the morgue to sign for the body." Oh great, another delay in getting my well-deserved beer. I filled out my flight paperwork (I had flown seven and a half combat hours that day for one combat mission counter) and hopped in the ambulance with the medics to head to the morgue.

After about an hour, the medics told me I could go because they had completed the identification of the body. Out of curiosity I inquired as to the name of the pilot I had just flown in from the field. The medic retrieved some paperwork and told me the name of the pilot… Captain James V. Newendorp. When the medic saw my reaction, he said, "Lieutenant, you OK?" I could barely speak. Jim Newendorp had been the very same instructor pilot that recommended that I take the FAC assignment with the promise of a follow-on fighter aircraft. I had flown many times with him at Reese Air Force Base in Lubbock, Texas in the T-37 in the fall of 1969. Captain Newendorp was one of the best pilots I had ever flown with during my short career, and he had been a real role model for me. I was totally beside myself. Rather than stopping at the club for a beer, I walked straight to the base chapel, got on my knees, and thanked the Lord for getting me safely through this self-inflicted crisis; I also prayed that Captain Newendorp's family would be OK. I have tried to recall all the promises that I made to God that night, like pray every day, read the Bible and all those things I promised. Have I kept all those promises? Hardly, but I am working on them.

As a side story to this infamous flight, I finally tracked down the family of Jim Newendorp in July 2008 when I was working on a FAC memorial that was built in Colorado Springs. His mother, five brothers and sisters, wife, son, and daughter were still alive. Most of the family lives in Iowa but his daughter, who was two years old when her father was killed, lives in Golden, Colorado. They invited me to a family reunion in Golden to fill them in on the details of his final flight. The Air Force didn't have much information to pass on to the family about his death, only the date and type of aircraft he was flying. The family was very pleased that I took the time to meet with them and relate the death of Captain Jim Newendorp.

The family also celebrated the 40th Anniversary of Jim's death with another reunion at the Air Force Academy in October 2011. Jim was a 1965 Air Force Academy graduate and his remains are buried at the Air Force Academy cemetery. At the reunion there were squadron mates of his who flew the RF-4 with him in Southeast Asia as well as his Air Force Academy roommate. I was able to once again relate the story of Captain Newendorp's last flight and hopefully add another chapter of closure for Jim Newendorp's family and friends.

I did fly another CSAR mission that was also very close to my heart between August 12-15, 1971. I was flying as a Pretzel FAC in support of the MACVSOG mission out of out of Bien Hoa and Quan Loi. After returning from a flight in the early afternoon I noticed that the mood in the FAC hooch was very low. I asked one of the Rash FACs what was up. He stated that one of their Rash OV-10 FACs, John Rydlevich, another young lieutenant, was missing and did not return after his late morning mission. Now this was really a problem for all of us in the hooch because John's wife was actually visiting him in Vietnam. She was a schoolteacher in Thailand and had come for the week to visit John. Since none of us lieutenants had ever dealt with such a touchy situation before, we got a hold of the Rash ALO and asked him to inform John's wife that he was missing in action. While that notification was going on the rest of the FACs in the hooch decided we needed to start a CSAR effort to find John or his wreckage.

We all headed down to the flight line and met at the squadron operations building to determine what aircraft were available to fly and what pilots still had the necessary crew rest to fly a CSAR mission. We also coordinated with the Rash operations center to get at least a starting point for the search. Rash Ops stated that John was scheduled to fly a VR mission that afternoon in an area about sixty-five miles to the northeast of Bien Hoa. We pulled out our maps and decided that we would prepare a search pattern with the aircraft and pilots we had available. The O-2 that I had just returned was in for maintenance and the rest of the 0-2 Pretzel FACs were already airborne on other missions. So, I decided that I would fly in the back seat of an OV-10 as a second set of eyes for the search. As I described earlier, we were assigned a box area of about fifteen square miles to search. The pilot in the front seat found a prominent location, a bend in the river, to start the search pattern. We flew at around 1,000 feet over the heavily jungled area. Back and forth we flew, sometimes getting down to around 500 feet to ensure we had good visual contact with the ground and the tree canopy. In spite of nearly three and a half hours of flying over the suspected crash site, we found nothing of interest and, because it was getting close to sunset, we returned to Bien Hoa and debriefed with all the other FACs that were looking for John. John could not be found.

The next day my 0-2 was flyable and, before taking off on a Pretzel VR mission, I flew another search mission in the area we suspected John was located. Still no contact from me or from the six other Rash FACs that were searching. Finally, on the third day, August 15, a 25th Infantry Division helicopter noticed a small brown area in the jungle; flying at tree top level they saw the crash site of an OV-10. Still not certain if this was John's crash site, our squadron Flight Surgeon boarded an Army helicopter and was dropped off at the crash site. Doing some forensic investigation, our Flight Surgeon determined that the body at the crash site was in fact that of John Rydlevich. The tail number observed at the crash site also matched the tail number of the OV-10 that John was flying.

The Air Force Joint Personnel Recovery Center later determined that John's aircraft had been shot down. We never really got an update on how John's wife reacted to the news or what happened to her following the crash. I guess at this early point in my Vietnam tour I was starting to harden to the fact that I would lose people that I knew well, but I had to just press on as there was always another mission to fly.

Kratie Prison Mission: Another unique and challenging mission that I flew was in support of an attempted prisoner of war (POW) rescue mission near the prison outside the Cambodian town of Kratie on the Mekong River. As I have described before, Kratie was a hot spot for enemy activity and a major staging location for NVA/VC supplies. There was a well-developed, years-old, concrete-walled prison located roughly four kilometers to the east of Kratie. The Pretzel FACs routinely flew over the prison and did visual reconnaissance every time we flew near or over Kratie. We also flew many High Low missions near Kratie.

On one such High Low mission our low bird was able to take a photo of someone in the center courtyard of the Kratie prison waving what looked like a white tee shirt at the FAC. After the photo was developed, it was determined that, in fact, there was someone in the center courtyard of the prison waving something white at the aircraft. This information was passed along to the SOG headquarters for action. It was well known that at least thirteen U.S. troops were missing and potentially held captive by the NVA/VC during the U.S. invasion of Cambodia in May of 1970. The thought was that perhaps there could be an American prisoner still confined in the Kratie prison. The actual organization that conducted all suspected POW rescue missions was the Joint Personnel Recovery Center (JPRC). While officially part of SOG, the JPRC acted independently from the SOG for the most part but exclusively used the SOG teams for the POW rescue missions. These POW rescue missions had the code name Bright Light.

The Pretzel FACs were ordered not to fly near the prison while a rescue plan was being put together by the SOG headquarters. We did not want to give any indication that we were interested in the prison. About four days later we got indications that a rescue mission would take place during the nighttime hours of September 22. The mission would involve a team of three U.S. Special Forces members, two Montagnard Special Forces, and one Vietnamese Special Forces soldier conducting a high altitude, low opening (HALO) drop near the prison before proceeding to the prison to attempt a rescue if there were American prisoners there.

In a HALO jump the team exits the back of C-130 at anywhere from 13,000 to 18,000 feet and delay opening their parachutes until much closer to the ground. The jumper would stabilize his fall and maneuver (fly) for about one minute, open the chute at around 2,500 feet, and then descend for another two and a half minutes, flying the parachute to the designated drop zone. The concept was if the drop aircraft was high enough, the enemy on the ground would not know an activity was taking place in their area. My part of this HALO mission that night was to be the radio relay for the dropped team so the team could communicate through me to SOG Headquarters. The weather was less than perfect, but I did get a call that the C-130E from the U.S.A.F. 20th Special Operations Squadron had taken off from Saigon and the drop mission was on. The planned drop was to be from 13,000 feet and I would be orbiting well to the south at 3,500 feet.

My take off time was 0100 from the very dark Quan Loi runway. The drop was scheduled to occur at 0200, and I was to attempt radio contact with the team as soon as they all landed and had regrouped as a team.

The planned landing zone was about 750 meters to the southeast of the prison. The plan was to keep in radio contact with the team throughout the night and then extract them from a pre-selected LZ to the southeast of the prison after the mission was complete. My schedule was to fly until 0600 and then be replaced by another FAC, Pretzel 03. I never did see the C-130 because of the weather in the area, but I did get a call that the drop had occurred at 0207 and that SOG was just waiting for radio contact. Still not wanting to give their position away, I stayed as far from the prison as I thought I could and still be within radio range for the team. Finally, at 0310 I got a call from the assistant team leader known as One One on the ground. He said the team leader known as One Zero had been badly injured during the jump and he was still attempting to locate two of his other team members. Apparently, they had become separated during the jump. I advised the SOG folks of the current status and was told to stay on scene until the ground team leader found all his team and decided on a course of action. Around 0400 I got a call that the One Zero and one of the allied SF troops were unable to continue due to injuries sustained in the HALO drop. I relayed this information back to SOG headquarters and was immediately informed that the mission was an abort and to move the team to the primary extract landing zone.

The SOG headquarters was already in the process of putting the extract team together and wanted to get the team out at first light. I got a visual contact with the team via a red strobe light and informed the team that they were approximately one kilometer from the briefed primary LZ. I informed One One they should head in a southeasterly heading to get to the LZ. After further discussion with One One he informed me that the team could get to the LZ in about forty minutes as there were no enemy forces trailing them at the time and they needed to assist the injured team members. With one final radio check and strobe light contact, I informed One One that the LZ was approximately one hundred meters on a heading of 135 degrees. The extract package consisted of two H-34 Kingbees and two Cobra gunship helicopters. Since the distance from Quan Loi to the LZ was only about fifteen miles I expected the helicopters to arrive at the LZ right at dawn. I was orbiting at around 2,500 feet at the time and got a good visual on the helicopters. I marked the LZ for the lead helicopter and Kingbee 27 said he had a visual on the LZ. The extract went off without a shot being fired at the rescue team or any shots from the attack helicopters. While the rescue mission was a failure, we did get the team out of harm's way. I don't believe this mission on the Kratie prison was ever completed, at least not during my time in Southeast Asia.

Chapter 9
OTHER VERY UNIQUE EVENTS DURING MY WAR

Barbecue Fireworks: One of the things that kept me sane during my year of combat were the many humorous activities that took place both in Quan Loi and back at the main operating bases of Ben Hoa and Tan Son Nhut AFB in Saigon. It almost seemed like a fraternity atmosphere as many of the FACs were in their early twenties, including me. One of the most amusing and, looking back now, dangerous activities was the newcomer orientation to the barbecue grill at our Bien Hoa FAC hooch. We called the newcomers "f*@^ing new guys" or FNGs. There were two FAC units in the same hooch: the Rash FACs that supported the U.S. 1st Cavalry Division and the Pretzel FACs that support the MACV SOG mission.

Since Bien Hoa was very close to one of the largest Army bases, Long Binh, we were able to buy some creature comforts at the very large commissary there as well as vast quantities of alcohol at the Class Six store at Long Binh. Beer and whisky shots in the hooch were ten cents each and each FAC kept a running total on a large sheet of paper behind the bar so we could pay up at the end of the month and buy more alcohol for post-flying activities. Occasionally we could purchase steak, hot dogs, and hamburgers at the commissary. Sometimes the commissary even carried charcoal for the barbecue grill that we had in the back of the hooch. One item that they very seldom, if ever, carried was charcoal lighter fluid. Being the inventive FACs we found a sure-fire way to light the barbecue grill.

According to tradition the FNG FAC in the hooch had the responsibility to get the fire going in the barbecue grill. The first obvious question was, "Where is the lighter fluid to start the fire?" The standard answer was, "We don't have any lighter fluid, but we have a backup source." We would direct the FNG to take a bar shot glass, about a three-ounce glass, go out to one of the jeeps, and put their arm and glass down the refueling tube on the jeep to fill up the glass with gasoline, and bring it back to start the fire. At the time, it seemed like a reasonable thing to do. Unbeknown to the FNG, one of the old FACs had already primed the barbecue with another glass of gasoline. The gas fumes were everywhere and when the newcomer slowly poured his gasoline on the barbecue grill and carefully lit the fire, there would be a massive explosion. The results were often hilarious with lost eyebrows, mustaches, and, occasionally, the front three inches of the FNG's hair line. Nobody was ever seriously injured in this stunt but looking back that was a pretty stupid tradition, to say the least.

Emergency Surgery: We were fortunate to have our 19th Tactical Air Support Squadron (TASS) Air Force Flight Surgeon living in our hooch. It was so convenient to have Doc available for any number of small medical issues that would normally come up during war time. It was sure nice not to take yourself off the flying schedule and wait to see the flight surgeon at the medical clinic at Bien Hoa. We considered Doc just one of the boys and he routinely partied very heavily with the FACs in the hooch. There were times that we didn't want to go to the Doc for a medical issue because he was in no condition to give us any rational medical advice.

One such incident really showed the flexibility of the FACs. Late one evening, one of the FACs fell off a bar stool in the hooch and, while trying not to spill his drink, managed to fall directly on the glass he was holding, cutting his left hand very deeply between the thumb and first finger. We immediately sought out Doc for help. When Doc came to the bar, we could tell he had way too much to drink but was alert enough to realize the hurt FAC needed stitches for the very large cut on his hand. So, four of us, including Doc, the hurt FAC, Ed Hooker, another Pretzel FAC, and I hopped in one of the squadron jeeps and drove to the medical clinic.

It was around 2:00 am and the clinic was closed, so Doc opened the clinic and we went into one of the exam rooms for the sutures. Ed and I could both see that Doc was in no condition to put in the sutures. So, we volunteered to assist under the direction of Doc. First, Doc told us we needed to numb the hand. Ed was going to do that part, so after Doc filled a syringe with some kind of local anesthesia Ed proceed to put the syringe into the cut area of the hand. Unfortunately for the hurt FAC, Ed put the syringe in way too far and as he pressed the plunger the anesthesia came flowing out the bottom of the hand and on to the exam table. He had inserted the syringe all the way through the hand. We all got a good laugh out of that procedure as we were all about four sheets to the wind.

Since I had an early morning flight, I was the "soberest" of the four of us and was designated to do the actual stitching. Because of the anesthesia and the drunkenness of the hurt FAC, I was able to put in about twelve very ugly sutures. The bleeding had stopped by now, and we all had another good laugh as we headed back to the hooch in the squadron jeep. It was a good thing the security police didn't stop us on our trip or we all would have been cited for DUI. The hurt FAC returned to the clinic later that morning and I am sure the medical staff on duty asked who in the hell did those stitches.

Malaria Prevention: One item that was briefed to us upon arrival in Vietnam was the prevalence of malaria in Southeast Asia. The mosquito population in Vietnam was prolific, and you could expect to get many bites on any given day. The U.S. military did have a plan to combat malaria. Upon arriving at Bien Hoa, I was ordered to take a very large orange pill each week and on the same day of the week during the entire time I was in Vietnam. The pill, acloriquine-primaquine-phosphate, was kept in bottle on each and every table in the chow hall, and readily available in our FAC hooch bar. While the pill did keep malaria away from me, it did have some very terrible side effects. Usually I took my weekly dose every Wednesday but after about three hours I would get the most unbearable case of the explosive "runs" I had ever experienced. So, I had this plan to try not to fly within the three-hour critical window after taking the malaria pill.

Well that plan worked for a while until my schedule was interrupted by an Issue FAC that was very sick. I was designated to take the flight for him about one hour after I took my weekly malaria pill. The first hour and a half of the flight went OK but soon after that point the boiling in my gut became unbearable and my bowels literally exploded in my flight suit. I was in the middle of a very intense air strike mission and did not have the option of returning to base after the explosion. To give the crew chief a break from having to clean up too much after this biological event, I slipped my plastic-coated main map under my ass to keep some of the poop off the seat cushion. I could feel the goo sliding down my leg as I pulled G's, maneuvering to keep the ground target and the fighters in site. The burning in my ass was almost unbearable and I couldn't wait for this mission to be over.

After about another hour and a half of flight, I headed back to base. By this time, I wasn't sure if I could make it back for a safe landing. I finally did land and as fast as I could I headed back to the hooch to get cleaned up a bit. One of the old FACs saw me enter the building walking very funny. He laughed and asked, "Download in flight?" I answered yes and he told me to just get straight into the shower with my flight suit and boots on and take care of the mess. Our mamasan, or hooch maid, was in the bathroom cleaning the sinks when I entered the room. She giggled as I went directly into the shower and stayed there for a good twenty minutes trying to clean myself up from the malaria pill explosion. I am happy to announce that was the last time that a little orange malaria pill almost brought me down. I watched my schedule much closer and never flew within three hours of my malaria pill on Wednesday mornings. Sometimes the malaria pill waited until later in the week.

Preflight Your Survival Water Bottle: A very funny occurrence happened at the Bien Hoa FAC hooch one flying day. It was common practice that each FAC would fill one or more olive green plastic survival water flasks with water and place them in the freezer compartment of the hooch bar refrigerator each night before flying. In the morning we would retrieve our flasks and start our daily flying missions. Usually by the time we were in our first hour or so of flying the water in the flasks had melted enough that we could drink it and at least try to stay hydrated in the hot and humid Southeast Asia weather.

On this particular day, one of the Rash FACs had a very huge surprise when he tried to drink his water from the survival flask. His immediate reaction was, "Damn! That is vodka in the flask!" He was obviously not too pleased with this development and looked at the flask and realized that he had taken another FAC's flask on this flight. As soon as he returned to the hooch he notified the Rash ALO of the incident and the ALO started an investigation of this problem. It seems that one of the older FACs, a former B-17 tail gunner from WWII, had been freezing his two water flasks filled with vodka for some time. We other FACs always wondered how this FAC could get so inebriated so quickly each night after his flying was completed. Needless to say, the older FAC was immediately taken off flying status and I don't believe he ever flew another FAC mission while I was at Bien Hoa. My survival water flask preflight took on new meaning after this incident and I doubled checked every morning that I indeed had my own water flasks.

Death by Gas: As I mentioned before most of the FACs in Vietnam were young lieutenants just a couple of years out of college. We were essentially like a big fraternity doing crazy things in the air and on the ground. One of the more humorous events was the almost perverse game to see who could pass gas the best. One evening after flying I was walking down the hall and heard some very gregarious laughter coming from one of the FAC rooms. I slowly opened the door and noticed the lights were off and there was a terrible smell in the room. I then saw the most amazing thing a naive boy from Oregon had ever seen: a couple of FACs on the top bunk lighting their farts on fire. You could see a bright bluish flame come out of the secret hiding place and the FACs were betting to see who could fire off the longest or brightest flame. I heard someone say be careful and only light the gas on the expel portion of this biological event.

The lighting portion of the activity became just too dangerous for this event to continue so we started another milder gas event in the hooch. We began a weekly contest where we would determine who could let the loudest and or smelliest fart in the building. We all had pretty good results with this event until Captain Bob Johnson, the Pretzel Operations Officer, arrived on scene. He asked, "What are you guys doing?" And we replied that we were grading FAC farts. He then said ok and let go with the loudest, most putrid fart we had ever experienced. You see, Bob Johnson had an affinity for egg salad, and he must have eaten four to five egg salad sandwiches a week which put him in the world class category of the unchallenged and undefeated FAC farter at Bien Hoa.

No T-shirts Allowed: I'm not sure where this tradition came from, but we had a rule in the FAC hooch that nobody could wear any clothing that showed an undershirt under your top shirt. It was not unusual for two or three folks a night to lose their T-shirts to the crazy FACs in the Rash/Pretzel hooch. The way it worked was as soon as a Rash or Pretzel FAC saw somebody with the T-shirt showing they would approach the individual and forcibly rip the T-shirt off the individual. It really didn't matter if they protested, the T-shirt was coming off. Usually it wasn't a problem if you were wearing a flight suit but a big problem if you were wearing a buttoned upper shirt or fatigue top.

One evening an Army full colonel was visiting one of the ALOs in the building and made the mistake of coming into the bar with a green T-shirt showing. Since there was no exception for anyone wearing a showing T-shirt, he immediately lost not only his T-shirt but all the buttons on the front of his starched military fatigue uniform. While we all thought it was funny, the Colonel and the ALO just didn't seem to catch the humor of our tradition. I believe the tradition was still alive when I moved to another base in the fall.

Wash My Jeep: Even though we were engaged in a day-to-day life or death war, there were many things that belied that setting. One of the areas that really upset the FAC community was the Army had a rule that they would not let us go through the government gas station and fill our tanks with gas until we washed all the dust and mud off our jeeps. Being the resourceful FACs that we were, we felt that requirement to wash the jeeps before refueling was complete BS and came up with a new plan to fuel our jeeps.

Chapter 9

While I assumed the normal jeep gas was around eighty-five octane, we decided that we could just as easily put aviation gas (AV gas) into our jeeps. But the aviation gas was 130 octane. Boy, did our jeeps perform on that high-octane gasoline. It seemed like we were driving high performance sports cars and we were lucky the security police did not have radar guns at Bien Hoa. The problem was the octane was so high that we managed to burn up the engines of two of our FAC jeeps after only a few weeks of driving with the high-octane gasoline. The Army was very confused as to why the Air Force FAC jeeps were burning up their engines at such a high rate. The bottom line was we didn't ever wash our jeeps again to fill up with gas.

Snake "Attack": One of the more interesting events that took place at Quan Loi was a snake scare in the Pretzel hooch. One of our FACs was returning to the hooch after an uneventful trip to the outdoor latrines. As he entered the hooch he noticed what he thought was a dark gray and white piece of a plastic door separator that we had leading from the great room in the front part of the hooch to the sleeping rooms in the back part of the hooch. After he had retrieved what he needed in his room, he came back to the great room and noticed that the strip of plastic that he saw on the floor was actually moving. He immediately recognized it as a Banded Krait snake, claimed to be the most poisonous snake in the world and a very common one in the area of Quan Loi. This snake had a very slim body and the one in the hooch was about four and a half feet long.

The Army troops called this snake a two stepper because after a bite you would only make it two steps before you died. I believe that description was somewhat of an exaggeration, but us killer FACs did not want to take any chances with that deadly visitor to our hooch. The first call, very loudly given, was, "SNAKE!"

All the FACs in the hooch, including me and a couple of Army helicopter pilots that were in the hooch, immediately pulled out whatever weapon we had handy. We all rushed to the back of the great room of the hooch and got a visual contact on the snake and began shooting our weapons—from my 38-cal. revolver to an AK-47 to multiple AR-15s. The snake was none too amused with our response and immediately retreated into one of the maintenance troop's rooms. We all continued with our flashlights shining toward to the back of the room and continued to blast away at the snake. We managed to completely destroy a stereo system, a footlocker, a pair of jungle boots, and an Army cot.

With all the gunfire coming from the Air Force hooch, some of our Army maintenance troops and a couple of SOF soldiers ran over to see what was going on. It was an absolute miracle that we didn't shoot each other as the bullets were flying throughout the hooch. Just when we thought we had dispatched the snake it came slithering at lighting speed toward the front of the hooch and right between our legs heading for the front door. As we all jumped out of the way the snake made it to the front door and was about to depart the area when one of our Air Force maintenance troops responding to the gunshots was able to kill the snake with a shovel.

We all looked rather inept standing around with burning hot guns in our hands looking at the dead snake that almost killed us all. The crew chief that lost the stereo system was none too pleased with the outcome, but what the heck this is war! This encounter firmly cemented my plans to never get into the bomb shelter just outside the hooch.

Cerano the Monkey: Toward the end of my time in Vietnam all the Pretzel pilots were transferred to a base in the Central highlands of Vietnam called Ban Me Thuot (BMT). It was about eighty air miles from Quan Loi but because the enemy action around Quan Loi had increased to a very unsafe level, we would spend the night at BMT with our aircraft, fly them to Quan Loi at first light, fly missions throughout the day and early evening from Quan Loi and then return to BMT for the night. And then do it all again the next day. The asphalt runway at BMT was 5,900 feet long, had a control tower, runway lights, and a navigational aid called a Tactical Air Navigation (TACAN) beacon.

BMT was located at approximately 1,760 feet above sea level so at times the nights would cool down very nicely. BMT was the location of the headquarters of all SOG activity in the southern part of Vietnam, all of Cambodia, and parts of Laos. The headquarters was known as Command and Control South, or CCS. Two other SOG headquarters, Command and Control Central, or CCC, was located in Kontum, South Vietnam, and Command and Control North, CCN, was located in Danang, South Vietnam. Another group of FACs, the Mike FACS, were also stationed at BMT and they had a rather "first class" operation there complete with air-conditioned rooms, a very nice hooch bar, and other amenities that we did not have at Quan Loi.

One of the unique things the BMT FACs had was a pet monkey for a mascot. The monkey, named Cerano, was a little brown monkey that loved to drink beer and run around in the hooch bar. There was a tradition in the bar for any FNG visiting for the first time. The scenario went like this: if the FACs knew a new person was entering the bar, they would grab Cerano by the nap of the neck and throw him across the room right at the new person entering the bar. Now most nights Cerano had already had too much to drink and as he flew through the air he would start s**tting. Just as he arrived at the unsuspecting visitor, a 10-pound monkey, followed by a stream of s**t would hit the newcomer right in the chest.

Since Cerano did not like this flying business he would grab onto the newcomer with both hands and hold on for dear life. It was very difficult to get him to let go but as the s**t started to smell it was not optional to keep a stinking monkey attached to your body any longer than necessary.

As time went on the Mike FACs felt sorry for Cerano and decided to get him a female companion. One of the maintenance folks went into the town of BMT and purchased a beautiful small female monkey as a companion for Cerano. It was humorous watching the two monkeys that they put together in Cerano's cage for the night. There was a lot of posturing from both of them and many strange sounds from each. Everyone was anxious to see how the two made it through the night. After I returned from another long day of flying at Quan Loi, I was informed that Cerano was found dead in his cage the next morning. Nobody was sure if the female killed him or if he was so amorous and he screwed himself to death. At any rate that was the end of the Mike FAC mascot.

High-Powered Hunting: After one insert mission I was flying above and behind some UH-1 Green Hornet helicopters around 500 feet. I was just keeping my eye on the landscape when I saw one of the helicopters dropping very low to almost ground level. I inquired of the helicopter if they had a problem. All I got was a call to stand by. I noticed the helicopter rapidly rotating around a very large row of bushes and then touch down in a small open space.

I was convinced that they had crashed, and I would have to start a CSAR mission to rescue the crew. Just as I got the Pretzel ops folks on the radio to activate the rescue forces the helicopter pilot called me and said that his crew had just shot a very large deer and had landed to pick it up to bring back to Quan Loi. What an amazing action. As the helicopter climbed back to 500 feet, I noticed the large deer in the back compartment of the Huey. It must have been quite the show shooting the deer with a fifty-caliber machine gun.

Once we landed back at Quan Loi, all the Quan Loi crew chiefs from both the Army and Air Force met the helicopter and loaded the deer into the back of their jeep. Once inside the compound they hoisted the deer to dress it. The plan was to send the deer meat to the chow hall to prepare it for the evening meal. Unfortunately, or maybe fortunately for me, I still had another flight to make that day and was not back to Quan Loi in time to enjoy the bounty of the jungle. I'm not sure if there were any more hunting trips during the remainder of my tour.

Beer Can Cannon: As I have stated before, the atmosphere among the FACs was like a fraternity, and we had many things to keep our minds off the war. Once we got back to the hooch at the end of the flying day all bets were off and, besides some very heated poker games, there was plenty of crazy activity. One of the "fun" things we did was make beer can cannons to shoot tennis balls at each other.

The mechanics of the cannon were simple. We would cut the top and bottom out of four beer cans and tape them together with duct tape resulting in a long hollow tube. We would then cut the bottom out of one more beer can and carefully cut about six holes in the top of the fourth beer can and then tape it to the long hollow tube of beer cans. Next, we put lighter fluid (when we had some) in the last can and shook the whole tube very briskly. Finally, we would put a tennis ball in the open end of the tube and got ready to fire the cannon. Firing the cannon was the simple lighting of the fumes in the cannon. The resulting explosion would propel the tennis ball the entire length of the building, "flying" down the hall at an extremely high speed. Whoever who stepped into the hallway just after ignition would have to try to dodge the flying projectile. We would shoot the cannon many times until we either ran out of lighter fluid or lost all the tennis balls. No one was ever severely injured by these cannon shots but a few unsuspecting FACs took a tennis ball to the crotch on occasion.

Ring Around the Rosie: During a High Low mission on July 14 I witnessed some more craziness from my brothers in arms. As we were progressing with the mission and had identified and marked twelve locations on my map, I saw the 0-1, call sign Aloft 14, start to make a 360-degree turn around a very large tree that was kind of in the open. I immediately armed my rockets and was prepared to fire as I thought the low bird had been hit by ground fire. A quick call to Aloft 14 got no response. My second call got a "stand by" response. I could see that the back-seat photographer was shooting his AK-47 out of the open window of the aircraft. I couldn't see what he was shooting at as I was having a difficult time keeping the low bird in site. I had to make a very tight 360 degree turn to say behind the turning 0-1 which was now below tree-top level.

I then got a call from Aloft 14 that said he had an NVA soldier trapped behind the large tree and was trying to get into position to shoot him. He must have made three turns around the tree before I got the call that the NVA had been neutralized. After landing we debriefed, and he said he had seen the NVA soldier leaning against the tree when they surprised him with their arrival. The soldier was so startled that he dropped his gun and was moving behind the tree each time the 0-1 got into position to shoot. This dance around the tree took three turns before the back seater was able to dispatch the soldier. The back-seat photographer said he was so busy trying to shoot his AK-47 out of the window of the maneuvering O-1 that he did not get any picture of his confirmed KIA.

Transfer from Bien Hoa and Tan Son Nhut: During my time in Vietnam our main operating base at Bien Hoa was changed twice due to operational needs of the military, I assumed. Our first transfer happened in mid-September when I arrived back to Bien Hoa for an overnight stay. Our ALO, Major Frank Leuck, told me that the entire home base operations of the Pretzels would be moving to Tan Son Nhut Air Force Base in Saigon and we had just three days to make that move. Never mind that we still had to fly all our sorties and operate out of Quan Loi. The only change would be we would do our seven-day cycle from the base in Saigon.

Now I certainly was not a fan of moving to Saigon where the headquarters of 7th Air Force was located. There was too much bureaucracy and not enough support for the troops in the field. Our living quarters were crammed into another hooch that we shared with a C-130 cargo squadron. The rooms were small but at least the air conditioners worked, and it wasn't too far to the Officer's Club. The one thing that I hated was that the C-130 squadron had a pet boa constrictor or python as a squadron mascot that roamed around the great room at will. I don't know how many times I came into the great room and found the six-foot snake wrapped around the TV trying to stay warm. I don't believe I ever stayed more than a few moments in that room when the snake was out "warming" himself.

The other thing I did not like about Saigon was all the rear echelon motherf**kers (REMF) that were always hanging around the club and the Base Exchange. REMFs were those officers that were not in combat, never had been in combat, and thought they ran the war. I remember one day I had just finished about five hours of combat flying in Cambodia and was on my way to the club for dinner when one of the REMFs, a lieutenant colonel, stopped me and told me one of my sideburns was too long and I needed to get a haircut immediately. "Yea, sure," was my response, "I will do it on my next down day and not before that as I have a 0500 flight the next morning." He thought I was being disrespectful and asked for my name and I wisely said, "Lieutenant Jones, sir."

Following our stay at Tan Son Nhut, the Pretzel FACs were once again moved on October 26, this time to Ban Me Thuot in the central highlands of Vietnam. We moved to BMT because the facilities at Quan Loi had been destroyed in a sapper attack and it was decided the pilots and airplanes could no longer safely spend the overnight at Quan Loi. Our maintenance and communication folks, however, still stayed the nights in Quan Loi. I will describe the evacuation of Quan Loi in another short story in these memories.

BMT was about eighty miles from Quan Loi but the accommodations were very good compared to Quan Loi and Saigon. We each had a separate room, with a locker and place to store our personal stuff and flying gear. The rooms had electricity and air conditioning. The food in the Army chow hall was passable.

The main drawback was the mud at BMT. In order to use the latrine or take a shower you had to get off the wooden walkway that was built in front of the FAC hooches and walk through the ankle-deep mud when it was raining or through the ankle-deep dust when it was dry (not very often). I learned a unique technique when taking a shower and walking back to the hooch from the shower: I showered with my underpants on then walked to the hooch with the still wet pants on and used them to clean my feet and ankles as soon as I got to the wooden walkway. I would then put the underpants in a basket for the mamasans to clean the next day.

Walking to the flight line was another challenge as the mud would build up on your boots and make for a very slippery time in the cockpit. During this move, which was completed on October 23, my call sign changed from Pretzel 06 to Mike 66.

Evacuation of Quan Loi: For many months the Pretzel FACs and the SOG troops operating out of Quan Loi knew that there was a tremendous enemy buildup just inside the Cambodian border. We had seen such increased activity that we knew an attack could come at any time. For nearly two months we had advised the SOG headquarters folks that there was a huge enemy build up near Quan Loi. In fact, we believed that the communist headquarters for the invasion of South Vietnam (COSVN) was located about six miles from Quan Loi. Despite repeated requests for air support to take out the COSVN headquarters, the staff at SOG refused our requests. We knew it was just a matter of time before we would be attacked.

Sure enough, in the very early hours of October 21, Quan Loi was attacked by approximately ten NVA sappers who placed nearly sixty satchel charges of high explosives around the buildings and flight line at Quan Loi. Our Pretzel FAC hooch took six direct hits, the photo lab was destroyed, the Army pilot's hooch was badly damaged, and the SOG team alert building was damaged. Fortunately, our outdoor latrines were left unscathed. All of our enlisted U.S.A.F. maintenance and communication troops were injured in the blast. One SVN soldier was killed and several more were wounded in the attack. Fortunately, the satchel charges that were placed near the flight line failed to explode. I must believe that our ALO knew that there was the possibility of an attack on Quan Loi as he had ordered our aircraft and pilots not to remain over night at Quan Loi starting on September 15.

All the Pretzel pilots at Tan Son Nhut got an early morning wakeup call and we gathered together to plan on how we would evacuate our troops from Quan Loi. Each pilot, there were five of us, and five aircraft would evacuate one of the enlisted troops and as much support equipment as we could safely carry in each aircraft. I made two trips to Quan Loi and back that day. A funny thing happened on my first trip back from Quan Loi. After I landed and taxied back to the parking area, I told the crew chief that I would be taking off as soon as I got all the support equipment off loaded from my airplane. I told him to just leave the airplane alone as it was working fine, and I wanted to take off immediately. While the last pieces of equipment were being taken off the aircraft, I had to pee really bad and I told the crew chief that I would be right back as I relieved myself just behind the metal revetment wall. I hopped back in the airplane and took off as soon as traffic permitted.

Once airborne I could not get my landing gear to retract. So I did a low pass over the tower asking them to check my aircraft for any damage. One of the tower operators said he had a good visual on my aircraft with his binoculars and saw a red lanyard flapping from the front gear. Damn, the crew chief put the landing gear pin back in the airplane while I was taking a pee and I didn't properly preflight my aircraft before takeoff. I felt really stupid, landed, went to the end of the runway, parked my airplane with the engine still running, removed the landing gear pin, and took off again.

Following the evacuation, we had a two-day stand down from operations at Quan Loi while the SOG folks figured out a plan to keep the site safe from further attack. I believe they brought in about seventy-five additional Yards to guard the site. That was the last time, however, that the FACs or the airplanes would spend the night at Quan Loi. We would operate and stay at BMT for the duration of the time I was in Vietnam. We would still fly out of Quan Loi every day but return to BMT each night. Our enlisted maintenance and communication troops, however, were sent back to Quan Loi to stay and support all our Pretzel operations.

Bureaucracy of War: I realized soon enough that even in a war there was a level of bureaucracy that had to be dealt with. Each one of the Pretzel lieutenants had duties assigned to us in addition to our daily flying requirements. I was the Pretzel

Instructor Pilot, the Pretzel Safety Officer, The Pretzel Functional Check Flight Officer, and the Pretzel Supply Officer. As the supply officer I was responsible for all the non-flying equipment and supplies at the Quan Loi operating location. This included all the hooch furniture, beds, mattresses, refrigerator, water heater (nonfunctioning as it was), and other various items in our possession.

I was required to conduct a quarterly inspection and inventory to report the location and condition of each item on my supply list. Needless to say, after the attack on Quan Loi most of the items on my supply list were destroyed in the attack. Our very wise master sergeant in charge of our aircraft maintenance advised me that I should ensure that those destroyed items were removed from my supply list or I would be liable for them when I left Vietnam. So, I got the Pretzel ALO and the Special Forces Site Commander at Quan Loi to sign a letter verifying all the items on my supply list that had been destroyed by enemy action. The sergeant also recommended that I keep a couple of copies of the two letters just in case I needed them when I out-processed from the war. Sure enough, in early December when I out-processed at Than Son Nhut I needed those two letters to clear my supply account. I learned from that lesson to always seek the advice of your enlisted troops…they run the Air Force.

Bored to "Death": After reading some of the very exciting and near-death missions I described above you may wonder if the adrenaline rush ever got old? We had a way to cope with this possible let down in feelings. During some very mundane and boring radio relay missions where we had to fly over the battlefield and be in position to be in contact with one of our teams, we had two aerial tricks that were exciting if not, in retrospect, very dumb. The first one involved using the local military newspaper, the "Stars and Stripes," for target practice in the air. If you carefully ripped the newspaper into a twelve-by-twenty-four-inch sheet and pushed that piece of paper out of the side window of the aircraft it made a perfect aerial target to try to fly through.

If the paper did not shred on making contact in the one hundred mile per hour or more air, it would open up to full size and gracefully float toward earth. Maneuvering the aircraft through the air attempting to hit the newspaper was a sure-fire way to deal with the boredom and get some of the adrenaline flowing again.

The second, and probably more stupid maneuver, was to see if we could launch a WP rocket straight up in the air, at precisely ninety degrees to the earth, to see how close the impact would be directly below our aircraft. The WP made a distinctive white flash on impact. It took very little brains to think about the consequences if we were successful. While the 0-2 was a fairly maneuverable aircraft, getting it to fly in a ninety-degree climb was nearly impossible. Not once in my thirty or so attempts to launch the WP at ninety degrees did the rocket ever actually launch at that angle. The resulting impact was always some distance away from my position in space. That was a good thing as it would have been very difficult for the Air Force to tell my family that their loved one had died shooting themselves down in Vietnam.

Instructor Pilot Check Ride: In early July Captain Bob Johnson, our Pretzel Operations Officer, asked me to get some right seat landing practice under my belt as he wanted me to become the Pretzel FAC Instructor Pilot (IP). So, for a couple of flights I hopped in the right seat with other Pretzel FACs and became proficient in right seat landings. I even changed seats on one of my solo flights so I could also get proficient in right seat operations including switch selection and rocket launches. I was very comfortable in the right seat as flying with the throttles in the left hand and the yoke/stick in the right hand was normal operations from the aircraft I had flown in pilot training.

My role as a Pretzel IP would be to check out new Pretzel FACs when they joined our team and ensure that all the Pretzels were conducting the mission properly. I also picked up the role of Functional Check pilot which meant that whenever certain maintenance was completed on an aircraft it had to be checked in flight to ensure the maintenance was completed properly. Because the Pretzel mission was so intense, all of the new Pretzel FACs joined our team after becoming combat ready in another FAC role. I never really had any problem with any of the new Pretzels checking out in our missions.

On the day I was to get my IP check ride from the Squadron Standardization and Evaluation (STANEVAL) pilot, I flew down to Bien Hoa following a mission in Cambodia for the check ride later in the afternoon of July 12. I was to meet the 19th TASS STANEVAL pilot, a major who I did not know. As I was waiting in the squadron building for the major, I heard the emergency announcement from the fire department that a 0-2 had crashed on the main runway at Bien Hoa.

I hopped in the squadron crew bus and went out to the runway to see what had happened. Oh my, it was an 0-2 that had got caught in wake turbulence from a landing C-130 aircraft. As I got near the airplane, I saw a major looking rather chagrined standing next to the damaged 0-2. I immediately recognized his name tag as the major who was to give me my IP check ride. Needless to say, I did not get my IP check ride that day and went back to Quan Loi only to return to Bien Hoa two days later for the real IP check ride that I passed with no problems.

Who Has Gas? As I mentioned earlier a lot of our off time was spent acting like crazy college students. Some of our U.S. special forces folks thought it would be "funny" if they introduced the Air Force pilots to something called chlorobenzylidene malononitrile (CS) gas, a type of tear gas. On a day that we had all completed our flying schedule we were just sitting around the Air Force hooch when one of the SOG troops threw a CS gas canister into our great room.

Now, I must explain what CS gas is. It is a very debilitating chemical that incapacitates almost immediately. Many types of tear gas and other riot control agents have been produced with effects ranging from mild tearing of the eyes to immediate vomiting and retching. In some cases, it can also cause an immediate and uncontrollable case of diarrhea. The chemical reacts with the moisture on the skin and the eyes, causing a burning sensation and immediate, forceful, and uncontrollable closing of the eyes. Other effects usually include tears streaming from the eyes, profuse coughing, nasal discharge that is full of mucus, burning in the eyes, nose and throat, disorientation, dizziness, and restricted breathing. The size of the CS solution droplets and the evaporation rate of the chemical determine the effect on the body. The most severe effects usually wear off in an hour or so, but some of the symptoms can last for many hours after the attack. CS gas is such an effective tool at incapacitating someone that our SOG troops did use this gas on some missions where they needed to incapacitate the enemy for a short time to retrieve a body or capture a key enemy figure without killing them.

Needless to say, the Air Force folks were rather pissed. After we had recovered, to a small degree, we were still puking and crapping in our flight suits, we returned the favor to the Army pilots' hooch and threw in two CS canisters. They were none too pleased either and came out of their hooch puking and swearing like a bunch of sailors. But this is not the end of the story. The Army folks really thought it was funny that the Air Force had gotten the first attack. They then decided that it would be even funnier if they threw a CS gas canister in the Vietnamese SF hooch so they could enjoy all the fun we had.

The problem was the that SVN SF Major had his family in the hooch, his wife and two small children. He was really pissed and came out of the hooch with his AR-15 blazing. I still don't know how none of the Army troops got shot during the major's response. This CS gas incident was certainly a topic of discussion at the next morning's operations briefing. Article 15 threats were abundant if it ever happened again. During my remaining months we never smelled as much as a whiff of CS gas at Quan Loi.

You Call, We Haul: One of the very unique missions the Pretzel FACs had was to haul whatever fit in our airplane to our forward operating location at Quan Loi. It really didn't matter what the item was, whether operating supplies, maintenance supplies, or personal use items, if it fit in the airplane, we would carry it. I can remember one flight carrying about one hundred cans of engine oil for the O-2. The cans were all nicely contained in two large cardboard boxes when I took off from Bien Hoa. However, by the time I landed in Quan Loi one of the cans was leaking very badly and I had a "river" of oil flowing into the cockpit area. At first, I was wondering why my feet were slipping off the rudder pedals. It was pretty exciting the last few minutes of the flight trying to keep my feet on the rudder pedals. The Quan Loi maintenance troops were none too pleased about cleaning up that slippery mess.

One of the other Pretzel FACs had a near disaster on one of his "cargo" flights. Our one and only government jeep at Quan Loi had a flat tire and we desperately needed to get a replacement tire to Quan Loi. So being a good Pretzel FAC, he loaded the tire in the back of the airplane and took off from Bien Hoa. The story goes that during flight he encountered some major turbulence and the tire somehow got airborne in the airplane, floated into the cockpit area, and got lodged right between his seat back and parachute. Needless to say, it was a very awkward place for the tire to land. The tire forced the pilot forward into a bent position, and he had a very difficult time controlling the airplane. Two of the most unique hauling missions I flew were during one of our in-county rest and recuperation (R&R) change-out flights. Our ALO had worked out a deal with the Rustics FACs that flew out of Ubon, Thailand that would allow a Pretzel FAC to spend a couple of nights of R&R in their FAC hooch. We would fly to Ubon and change out with a Pretzel FAC that was already there enjoying his R&R. The returning FAC would take the airplane, fly a mission enroute, and return to Quan Loi. The flight to Ubon was only about an hour and a half long but we always flew a mission enroute to and from Ubon.

My inbound flight to Ubon was on July 23, and it was during this flight that I almost got shot down. One of the most unique locations in the world is the ancient Buddhist temple complex of Angkor Wat. It was built in the early 1100's and the complex covered an area of almost 400 acres. The main temple building was surrounded by a nearly two-mile-long water filled moat. Angkor Wat is "kind of" on the route to Ubon if you fudged a bit. It was very easy to find the main temple building complex because of the moat. I knew there were flight restrictions over Angor Wat, but I was a fearless lieutenant. As I flew down to about 500 feet to get a good view of the temple and take as many photos as I could, I saw a huge barrage of .51 caliber anti-aircraft fire aimed at my aircraft. With some very skillful hard maneuvering I was able to depart the area without taking a hit. I did, however, get some very good photos of the temple complex.

Once in Ubon the normal routine was to go into town and visit three places: first, the tailor shop to get my FAC party suit measured and ordered, next to the shoe store to get my custom-made Wellington boots measured and ordered, and finally to a Thailand gift shop to order some unique trinkets. While we visited each shop, we picked up the stuff that the previous Pretzel FACs had ordered and we then returned that stuff to Quan Loi. On my visit to the gift shop the owner of the store told me he had some items that I needed to take back to a previous Pretzel FAC that had visited the shop a few weeks before. What he had ordered were four very large painted ceramic elephants that would act as part of the shelving for his stereo system. Each elephant was very heavy and about twenty-four by twenty-four inches. The shop owner called for a taxi as there would be no way that I could carry these elephants back to the base on my own. I was able to get the taxi driver on base, and I off loaded the elephants, the completed party suits, and boots to take back to Quan Loi. The rest of my time in Ubon was spent just resting and eating some very fine meals at the Officer's Club. When it was time to return to Quan Loi, I was very concerned about how I was going to get all that stuff I picked up into my aircraft. With the help of a crew chief I was able to stuff all the items into the rear and right seat of the aircraft. My airplane looked like something right out the Beverly Hillbillies move to California. I had no way to tell how much those damn elephants weighed.

I sure hoped I could get and stay airborne with all the stuff jammed into my airplane. I guess I should have known something was amiss when it took me almost 6,000 feet to get airborne from the 10,000-foot Ubon runway. The airplane was very sluggish and hard to control. With the elephants in the back of the airplane I had a very aft center of gravity. I was sure praying that my return flight on July 25 did not involve an air strike mission that required a lot of maneuvering. Fortunately, it was a simple radio rely mission with one of our inserted teams. After a nearly two-hour flight I landed at Quan Loi and wanted to place those elephants you-know-where in my fellow Pretzel FAC. These two flights convinced me that I was flying a bit on the edge if I wanted to safely complete my tour in Southeast Asia.

Bless Me Father for I Fly: I was not a very religious person during my time in Southeast Asia. However, knowing some of the risks I faced each day convinced me that I should attend church whenever I had the opportunity. For me that meant whenever I was at Bien Hoa or Tan Son Nhut on a Sunday I would attend Mass. After one of the services I was talking about the mission I was flying as a Forward Air Controller with one of the Air Force Catholic chaplains. He appeared very interested in our mission and asked many questions about exactly what we did, at what altitude we flew our missions, and where we were stationed. I thought he had a real interest in what we did. He asked me if I thought it would be OK if he came to our flight line and blessed our FAC aircraft to help ensure we all returned from our missions safely.

I really didn't think that would be a problem and invited him to come by our Pretzel hooch after the second Mass so I could escort him to the flight line. He still wore his Catholic Mass robes when he picked me up around 1230 in the afternoon. He also had a small kit with him that I assumed carried holy water or something like that. As we got out of his jeep near the 0-2 parking area, he opened up his small kit and brought out a silver scepter looking tool. He said a few prayers to keep us safe and then sprinkled the holy water on the four adjacent 0-2s. Wow, did I ever feel that I would never be in danger again on any of my future FAC missions. So certain the prayers and holy water would protect us, I asked the Chaplain if he would like to fly a mission with me the next morning. His answer was immediate, "Hell no, I could get killed." So much for the power of prayer and the application of holy water. In spite of this "religious" experience, I did attend Sunday Mass whenever I was near a Catholic chapel for the rest of my tour.

Circus Time: After we transitioned to the base at BMT we had the opportunity on our return flights from Quan Loi to fly over some absolutely spectacular terrain in the central highlands of South Vietnam. The terrain was a lush, almost completely covered jungle canopy with many streams and waterfalls flowing through the various canyons. You could only see the river and waterfalls in certain areas where there was some clearing. On one of my many flights back from Quan Loi I was flying at just tree top level enjoying the beauty of this area of Vietnam when I was convinced that I saw a very large cat in a clearing by the river. I was so startled that I did an immediate 360-degree turn and, sure enough, there was a huge tiger sunning himself on some very large rock outcroppings near the river. The tiger barely raised his head as I flew directly over him. As I was maneuvering to get some pictures of this incredible find, he very slowly got off the rocks and walked directly back into the jungle. After I landed, I asked one of the Vietnamese lieutenants if what I saw could be possible. He told me there were many tigers known to be in the area just to the west of BMT. What a find!

On one other treetop flight back to BMT I spotted something just as inspiring as the tiger: a herd of elephants. There were five elephants walking in a row through a clearing just to the west of one of the many rivers that flowed through this area of Vietnam. At first, I thought I had come upon a pack of wild elephants but on further inspection I saw some very colorful cloth like material around the necks of two of the elephants. I had to assume that they were being used by the locals to haul things around in the jungle. We did know for a fact the NVA used elephants to carry war supplies in this part of Vietnam to the front lines for their eventual invasion of South Vietnam in 1972 and then again when they overthrew the South Vietnamese government in 1975. These elephants were safe from attack on this flight as I did not see any troops around the elephants and, besides, we did have some restrictions on shooting elephants unless we could confirm they were carrying war supplies.

Radio, Dead on Arrival: On a flight in late September we were trying to get a replacement radio to one of our teams still in the field. A radio for one of our SVN SF teams was not functioning properly and at the 0600 radio check they advised the FAC and the ride along interpreter that their radio was nearly unusable and would need another radio to complete the mission. Later that morning it was decided that we could drop a new radio to the team using a very rudimentary parachute system. Our SOG experts fashioned the parachute from a parachute left over from a flare drop. The plan was that I would fly very low over the team's position and have the SVN interpreter drop the radio to the team out of the right window of the 0-2, stay airborne to see if the replacement radio worked, and get an update on how their mission was progressing. The radio weighed about ten pounds, and the parachute was a homemade contraption that looked like it might work. I briefed the interpreter on exactly how he should drop the radio to the team. We even did a few simulated drops while we were still on the ground to ensure he had a clue about what he was doing. I got a thumbs up from the interpreter that he understood how he was to drop the radio to the team.

I took off in the early afternoon to drop the radio to the team. I found the location of the team, and they signaled me with a survival mirror so I knew their exact location. I found a fairly clear area about one hundred meters from the team's location to drop the radio because I didn't want the radio's parachute to get caught in the trees. I slowed to about seventy miles per hour and descended to about one hundred feet and told the interpreter to get ready to drop the radio. We had practiced placing the radio on the window ledge of the right window so he could steady the radio before forcefully throwing the radio down and away from the aircraft. My greatest concern was I wanted to make sure the radio cleared the rear propeller of the aircraft. I asked the interpreter if he was ready, and I got an affirmative head nod from him. I watched as he put the radio on the window ledge, and I was going to give him a countdown to drop so we could get the radio as close as possible to the team. Just as he lifted the radio to the window, we hit a bit of light turbulence and he dropped the radio out the window directly into the spinning rear propeller. The aircraft made a loud banging noise and the rear engine began to violently vibrate. Obviously, the radio was destroyed on impact with the propeller. Since I was so low and slow, I "nursed" the airplane into a climbing attitude and then feathered the rear propeller.

The 0-2 performance with just the front engine was marginal at best…but we were still flying. This was the second time I wanted to shoot the interpreter and kick his ass out of my airplane. As I turned back to Quan Loi, I was uncertain that I would make it back for a safe landing. My only goal was to land safely. There were no airfields between my location and Quan Loi. I just keep flying the aircraft and finally after a very tense thirty-minute flight I landed safely at Quan Loi. Inspection after landing showed that the rear prop was dinged, slightly bent, and out of balance from hitting the radio. We never again tried dropping a radio or any other supplies out of the window of the 0-2. Our resupply of the radio to the team was carried out by a helicopter drop very late in that same day.

Army/Air Force Flying Exchange Program: Usually over many beers the Army and Air Force pilots would exchange war stories and compare the aircraft each was flying. Occasionally we would offer to give each other a ride in our aircraft. I took three different Army 0-1 and helicopter pilots on flights with me. Most of their comments, at least from the 0-1 pilots, were that the 0-2 was too complicated compared to the 0-1 and had limited visibility for the side-by-side seating arrangement. Each Army 0-1 pilot I flew with handled the 0-2 with ease… not so much for the helicopter pilots.

I did have the same opportunity to fly "with" an 0-1 pilot and had a very exciting story that went with the flight. We went to the flight line to fly the 0-1, the Army pilot told me to strap in the front seat, and he would assist with engine start and preflight checks etc. After we got the engine started, I asked him if he was going to get into the back seat. He answered, "No, you will probably kill me." So being the impetuous lieutenant that I was, I decided I could fly the 0-1 with no problem. He did tell me I needed to fly the tail wheel off the ground as I had never flown a tail-dragging airplane before. I taxied to the runway, added power, and was able to make a fairly non-eventful take off. I climbed to about 1,500 feet and tried maneuvering the aircraft through its paces. No problem flying the aircraft and the visibility from the O-1 was superb. I certainly saw why the O-1 pilots did not like the visibility in the O-2.

Since there were no rockets on board, I flew for only about one hour and returned to Quan Loi for landing. The landing was where the fun began. Remember, I had never flown a tail dragger before and was really unsure if I needed to fly the tail to the ground or just let the aircraft land like the O-2. The touchdown was OK within the first fifty feet of the runway but as I slowed down, I obviously did not get the word about flying the tail to the ground. I did the most spectacular ground loop you have ever seen. The Army pilots and maintenance folks that were watching had a very loud and boisterous laugh as they came out to the airplane to see if I was OK. I really think they were more concerned about the aircraft than me. So much for my first and only flight in the O-1.

My next great joint flying adventure was two helicopter flights out of Quan Loi. The first flight was in a Cobra AH-1 Helicopter. The Cobra was a sleek, single-engine helicopter that was fifty-three feet long with a maximum takeoff weight of 9,500 pounds. It could reach speeds up to 150 knots. We got so much support during our insert/extract missions from the Cobras that I wanted to really understand how effective this helicopter was. The Cobra is a two-seat tandem arrangement helicopter with the pilot in the back seat and the copilot or the gunner in the front seat. I was strapped into the front seat and given a briefing on how to fire the multiple weapons on board the aircraft. The pilot said I could "fly" the bird after we got airborne and to a safe altitude. The visibility from the front seat was superb, and we leveled off at around 500 feet. The pilot walked me through the dynamics of flying a helicopter. My God that was ugly. I really had a very hard time coordinating the collective, the stick (cyclic), and the anti-torque pedals trying to keep the helicopter flying in a straight and level condition. Finally, the pilot said, "I got it," and took over flying the rest of the mission.

As soon as we were in an open area, we started the real fun, and that was firing all of the weapons on board. I started with one 40 mm grenade launcher that was housed in a turret under the nose of the helicopter. I next shot multiple rounds of 7.62 mm from the internally mounted gun and culminated my shooting by launching all thirty-eight 2.75 rockets mounted on short winglets on the side of the helicopter at an imaginary target on the ground. What firepower! I believe I was "Winchester" (out of ammo) in less than three minutes.

My second helicopter flight was in a very small and maneuverable OH-6 Observation helicopter. It was affectionately known as the Loach. It was a single engine helicopter with a maximum takeoff weight of 3,500 pounds and a maximum speed of 150 knots. The Loach was used for observation and command and control missions.

My pilot on the orientation flight was a nineteen-year-old warrant officer that was one wild and crazy guy. I had seen many Loaches flying nearly at ground level during my time in Vietnam. I didn't realize how low that was and how maneuverable the helicopter was. We zipped around the airfield at breakneck speed. I am sure the pilot was trying to scare the crap out of me…and he was nearly successful. After the flight I was very content flying my "boring" 0-2A.

Inflight Aircraft Emergencies: The 0-2 was a very reliable aircraft and I experienced very few aircraft malfunctions, not caused by ground fire hits, in my 750-plus hours of combat flying time in the airplane. One incident was very minor; the second one was rather challenging. I had flown the aircraft so much and could almost tell by feel what airspeed and altitude I was flying at without looking at my flight instruments. On August 17 I was taking off out of Quan Loi and was airborne for VR mission in Cambodia. Just as I got airborne one of the flight instruments caught my eye as the needle was moving in the wrong direction. I at first thought that one of my engines had rolled back but I did not feel any loss of power. Upon a closer look I saw my airspeed indicator moving in the wrong direction, in other words the airspeed was decreasing as I continued my climb out.

My flying instinct was that the aircraft was in fact accelerating and climbing normally. A closer look showed me the speed descending through about twenty miles per hour…not a speed that would keep me airborne for long. I continued my climb to a safe altitude and turned back toward the field. Doing a bit of maneuvering the airplane felt completely normal but as I increased power, the airspeed dropped even further to around ten miles per hour. I called Pretzel Ops and explained the situation and asked for the maintenance folks to be ready to meet my aircraft as soon as I landed. The turn back to Quan Loin and the lineup on the runway and landing felt completely normal. I taxied back to the parking area and shut down the engines.

The crew chief was waiting for me. I explained the situation with the airspeed indicator to him, and he seemed to know exactly what the problem was. He walked to the front of the airplane and was working on the pitot tube, which is a pressure measurement instrument that measures airflow velocity and senses the speed of the aircraft. He pulled a very large bug from the pitot tube and said that should fix the problem. I must have hit the bug on my initial takeoff roll and fouled up the pitot system in the airplane. My subsequent takeoff was completely normal, and the airspeed indicator worked as advertised.

My second inflight emergency was a little more complicated. I was finishing up on another VR mission on September 23 and had flown about two hours, had expended all of my rockets, and was in the process of returning back to Quan Loi when I had heard a very loud bang toward the rear of the aircraft and felt the airplane start to shake violently. I was convinced that I had taken a fairly large caliber hit to my aircraft and felt a terrible vibration coming from the rear engine. I did the standard response to any aircraft emergency that I learned in pilot training: maintain aircraft control, analyze the situation, and take corrective action. I felt the vibration was so intense that I immediately shut down the rear engine. Fortunately, the vibration stopped so I knew there was something wrong with the rear engine.

As I turned toward Quan Loi for a landing, I noticed that the elevator control on the airplane was non-responsive. An elevator on an airplane controls the pitch of an aircraft, allowing up or down motion of the aircraft. This was not a good situation. I was concerned that I would not be able to control the airplane to a safe landing. I had done a number of flight control checks in the 0-2 in my additional duty as a Function Check Flight (FCF) pilot after major maintenance on an aircraft. I slowly went through my options on what I should do. As I was maneuvering, I realized that I could control the pitch of the aircraft somewhat with the use of the trim tab on the back of the aircraft elevator. A trim tab is a small aerodynamic device that attaches to the trailing edge of the elevator allowing the pilot to control the stability of the aircraft as the speed and weight of the aircraft changes.

I called back to Pretzel Ops and asked to get a maintenance crew chief on the radio to explain the situation I was dealing with. He advised me that I should try to recover the aircraft at Bien Hoa or Tan Son Nhut as he did not feel he had the expertise or tools to deal with the flight control and or engine issue I was dealing with. I then turned toward Bien Hoa as it was the closest airfield, had crash recovery equipment available, and was less congested than Tan Son Nhut. I was still about eighty miles out and began reviewing my options for landing.

I determined that the best option was to fly a long, very shallow straight-in approach to Bien Hoa. I called Bien Hoa Tower and declared an emergency. While flying toward landing I tried various landing configurations and speeds to determine if I could in fact control the pitch of the aircraft to a safe landing. The airplane was reacting quite normally to my trim inputs and I lined up on about a five-mile very shallow final approach. I determined that I would use only partial flaps and a speed about ten miles per hour higher than normal to give some flexibility at touch down since the runway was 10,000 feet long. As I got close to the ground I made a final adjustment of full nose-up trim and the airplane made a rather firm but safe landing. I cancelled the emergency and taxied to the 0-2 parking ramp.

After engine shut down my aircraft was surrounded by the 0-2 maintenance team. On visual inspection we saw that something had hit the right tail boom of the 0-2 and had completely severed the control cables to the elevators. The tail boom was almost completely severed as well. An engine expert said he found the problem. The 0-2 engine propeller system has a counterweight on each side of the propeller that helps balance the propeller while spinning. One of the counterweights had come off the propeller and cut through the tail boom and the control cables. After reviewing how close the aircraft came to being shot down by the counter weight, I was more than ready for a beer.

Kingbee Mid-Air Collision: While this story could very easily fall under the CSAR missions that I flew, there is a component that is somewhat different. On October 10 Pretzel ops was notified that two of our Vietnamese H-34 Kingbee helicopters were missing on a flight from Quan Loi to Tan Son Nhut. Once again, the fall monsoon weather was terrible. I immediately joined in the search for the missing choppers. Pretzel 03, along with two 0-1's, Aloft 15 and Aloft 17, were also scrambled for the search. Since we knew the general direction the helicopters were flying, we found the wreckage of both helicopters fairly easily. It appeared that they had a mid-air collision with each other and crashed about a kilometer apart. Unfortunately, there were no survivors on either aircraft, and eight very brave airmen were killed. Once we returned to Quan Loi with the crash site location, the U.S. Special Forces members prepared to help retrieve the bodies of the eight airmen. It was such an amazing scenario listening to the Special Forces troops decide who would go to the crash site to retrieve the bodies. Since the Vietnamese helicopter crews were held in such high esteem and were respected so much for their fearless flying, the U.S. troops were pulling rank on each other to be among the six troops selected to retrieve the bodies. This kind of very special comradery was so obvious in each and every mission we conducted from Quan Loi. It didn't matter if the troops were Vietnamese, Cambodian, or Hmong, each member of the SOG team was respected, supported, and held in high esteem. And, as I saw on almost every single mission our SOG teams conducted, the team members were prepared to die for each other.

Tricked the System: As soon as I completed my Combat Ready Check in March 1971, I decided it was time to start planning for my follow-on assignment after Vietnam. I checked with many FACs that were approaching the end of their one-year tour to find out what kind of assignments they were getting. I certainly did not like what I heard. I remember the "promise" from the Air Force that if I took a FAC assignment I would be in a very good position to be assigned to a fighter aircraft after a tour in Vietnam. After two plus months of combat flying, I was so impressed by the autonomy and responsibility I was given as a young lieutenant FAC. I was cocky and just didn't think I wanted to fly in a multi-crew aircraft: fly straight and level and have the headquarters tell me exactly when I could fart or how I was supposed to fly. I had become a hard-core fighter pilot wannabe. Most of the post-Vietnam assignments the FACs got were B-52 bombers, KC-135 tankers, and few cargo planes. One FAC in about twenty got an Instructor Pilot slot in the T-37 at an undergraduate pilot training base. These were exactly the kind of assignments I did not want to happen.

On an off-flying day, I went to the Air Force Personnel Office and made the decision to put in a date of separation or DOS. This meant that once I left Vietnam I would have just two and a half more years of active duty service that I owed the Air Force. I had no particular plan in mind only that I did not want to fly a bomber, tanker, or cargo airplane. I would come up with a plan after I got out of the Air Force. The die was cast and I would only have to wait about six months before my follow-on assignment came down. Just as I predicted, I was assigned to a KC-135 tanker squadron at Lockbourne Air Force Base in Ohio with KC-135 training at Mather Air Force Base in California for six months before reporting to Lockbourne. I was none too pleased, but at least I would only have to fly that lumbering airplane for a short two and a half years. Once we got our orders to our follow-on assignments, we were officially in a FIGMO (finally got my orders) status. FIGMO usually meant a state of total indifference to the war. In my case however, I still had missions to fly and I wanted to be as sharp as possible to the end.

My fate was sealed, and I just continued flying missions almost every day waiting for the date in December for my transfer to Ohio. In mid-October my orders to Ohio were cut and I prepared a lot of my personal belongings to be shipped out in early November. I even had taken most of my personal items to the base transportation office to be shipped out. They were packed up and would arrive in Ohio when I returned from Vietnam.

One day in early November after I landed at BMT I had a message in the operations room to call back to the personnel folks at Bien Hoa about my assignment. It was too late in the day for the REMFs to be in the personnel office, so I called the very next morning. I got a hold of personnel staff sergeant and he told me that because I had put in a DOS I would not have enough time left in the Air Force to complete my additional commitment—two years extra for taking the assignment and one extra year for completing KC-135 school. Oh, what a shame! My new assignment would be to Eglin Air Force Base in Fort Walton Beach, Florida. I would be flying as a range safety officer, whatever the heck that was. By the luck of me putting in a DOS and avoiding the KC-135 assignment I eventually got to fly fighters in the Air Force, remove my DOS with a regular officer commission, fly fighters for another twenty years, and retire as a colonel. But that follow-on flying story is for another time.

Bombs Away: There was always a great amount of rivalry among the various flying squadrons in Vietnam, whether it was Air Force versus other Air Force squadrons or Air Force versus Army units. The rivalry could become intense. Many times, two FACs from different FAC units would challenge each other to a rocket shooting contest. Near Bien Hoa there were three flatbed rail cars that had derailed about five years prior. These rail cars were the targets and each FAC would shoot three rockets at the train cars. The closest to the cars would win and get free beer from the loser back at the hooch. One particularly intense rivalry was between the FACs in the Pretzel/Rash hooch and the A-37 pilots that lived in their own hooch. Our squadron buildings were side by side near the flight line. The A-37 squadron, the 604th Special Operations Squadron, had an inert 500-pound bomb mounted on a steel pole at forty-five-degree angle in front of their squadron building. The FACs, the 19th Tactical Air Support Squadron (TASS), had a large sign in front of their building with a painting of Snoopy flying a doghouse. Both the Rash and Pretzel FACs controlled many bombing missions by the A-37 Rap pilots, so the environment was ripe for competition.

One morning we arrived at the squadron building to see that a mustache and been mysteriously added to the painting of Snoopy. Not to be outdone, the Rash/Pretzel FACs decided it was time to "borrow" the MK-82 500-pound bomb from the A-37 Squadron building. One of our Pretzel maintenance troops got a portable welding torch, and we were ready to do our deed. Just as it got dark, six of us hopped in two FAC Jeeps and drove to the flight line. The crew chief met us in front of the A-37 building and fired up the welding torch. He made very quick work of the steel pole that held the bomb and it fell to the ground with ease. Now we had to figure out what do with the bomb as we did not know that the bomb was filled with concrete and it probably weighed a good 700 pounds. A MK-82 is a little over seven feet long, much too long and heavy to fit into a single Jeep. No problem—we used both Jeeps to move the bomb back to our hooch.

As ingenious FACs, we decided if we had one Jeep going one direction we could back the second Jeep up to the first and place the bomb on the back ends of both Jeeps. The only issue would be for the second Jeep to drive in reverse in close formation with the front Jeep. A large amount of alcohol really helped in our planning for this caper. The bomb only slipped off the Jeeps twice during our mile-long drive back to the FAC hooch. We were only stopped once by the Military Police. It was a good thing that both of the drivers were somewhat sober. Once we got back to the hooch, we had plenty of extra hands to transport the bomb right into our hooch bar and place it prominently in the corner of the room. We were so proud of our accomplishment. Two days later our Snoopy sign was missing but we still had the bomb in our hooch.

Old Swimming Hole: The Quan Loi Special Forces compound and the Quan Loi runway were built in the middle of an old French rubber plantation. The runway ran right through the middle of the plantation. The owner of the plantation, despite the war going on all around him, still lived in the mansion that he built prior to WWII. The old plantation home and grounds must have been spectacular in its day. It had a tennis court and a full-size Olympic swimming pool complete with a diving board and a bath house built on the side of the pool. Somehow either the Pretzel ALO or the Special Forces commander at Quan Loi convinced the owner to let some of the military personnel stationed at Quan Loi enjoy the unique pleasure of swimming in the pool.

The word got out that the pool would be open for one hour only on a very hot July day. Those of us that weren't flying gathered up our defensive weapons, our best pair of underpants and our towels and headed to the pool. Since the pool was near our compound, we all just walked through the deep red dust to enjoy ourselves. The Special Forces folks had one additional requirement…we all could not be in the pool at the same time. So out of the twelve troops that went to the pool, four of us took shifts, one on each side and each end of the pool with our weapons ready, just in case we offered the enemy a very lucrative target.

Now I must say the dip in the pool was quite refreshing even though the water was an avocado green. I am sure there had not been any pool chemicals in the pool since the sixties. Nevertheless, it was a good reprieve from the war, and I don't believe anyone got sick from our pool party. We never again had the pleasure of getting in the pool while I was still at Quan Loi.

Bad Timing: Following a very routine team insert on August 16 I was returning to Quan Loi in loose formation with two Cobra Helicopters when I passed Highway 13 about twenty-five kilometers east of the Cambodian town of Kratie. Right in the middle of the highway were three motorcycles, laden with supplies, travelling west toward Kratie. The cyclists did not see my aircraft as I descended to nearly tree top level to get a better look at the supplies and the riders on the bikes. As soon as the riders saw my aircraft, they exited the highway and all three of them dove into a culvert that ran perpendicular under the highway.

I immediately notified the helicopters to start an orbit in place as I had found a target of opportunity for them. I identified the culvert for the helicopter pilots and, being the good FAC, told them that I would mark the target for them as I still had seven high explosive rockets from an earlier High Low mission. Since these targets on the road were in a free-fire zone, I did not need clearance to engage them. I lined up for the rocket launch and aimed for the opening of the culvert on the south side of the highway. The rocket was placed in a perfect location and entered the opening of the culvert, and I saw debris exit on the north end of the culvert. This launch was probably my most accurate rocket launch during my entire tour.

Seeing the results of my rocket "marking" the target I advised the helicopter pilot that the target was neutralized with my rocket launch. I then pointed out the three motorcycles and supplies on the south side of the highway near the culvert and cleared them to destroy the motorcycles and supplies with whatever ordnance they had on board. They fired multiple 40 mm grenades, HE rockets, and 7.62 mm rounds. I then advised the helicopters of the BDA: three motorcycles, six large supply bundles, and three NVA KIA. It certainly was a target of opportunity and very bad timing for the three individuals carrying the supplies.

Fini Flight: There was a FAC tradition that when you made your last combat flight in Vietnam there was a wild celebration with all the folks in your unit. The fire department would meet your aircraft upon landing and spray you down with thousands of gallons of water, and your crew chief would meet you at the airplane with a bottle of champagne. The problem at Quan Loi was that we had neither a fire department nor access to champagne. So, we improvised. Another Pretzel FAC, Ed Hooker, who I had met in the Philippines during jungle survival school, was having his final Pretzel flight on the same day as mine. We both had missions to fly before our last flight, so we came up with a plan for our "fini" flight celebration upon returning from our missions.

Now we were both very aware that we didn't want to shine our asses too much on this fini flight as we both had flown around 500 combat sorties and survived; we did not want to be killed on our last flights. The first month I arrived in Vietnam an Air Force ALO had been killed on his fini flight in an OV-10 by flying too low for the maneuver he was trying to perform. He also killed the replacement ALO that was flying with him for a newcomer's orientation flight. That would not happen to us. Ed and I coordinated on the radio when we both had completed our first mission of the day. Ed had flown a VR mission, and I had flown a morning radio relay mission. We decided to join up west of Quan Loi at around 1,500 feet in a close formation and fly a low pass down the Quan Loi runway. We notified Pretzel Ops that we were inbound and all the pilots and maintenance crews from both the Air Force and Army that were not flying or working went to the airfield to celebrate our fini flight.

Ed and I both made numerous low-level passes down the runway both in formation and single ship. One of the crew chiefs lit off some colored marking flares for us to fly through. Upon landing the crew chief and other pilots met us both with a champagne substitute, a warm Schlitz beer. What an exciting tour I had. It was an honor to have flown with so many dedicated and talented people during my year in Vietnam. I made some lasting friendships that are still strong to this day.

DEROS: DEROS was just another one of the many acronyms that was used in this war and it meant Date Eligible to Return from Overseas or the date you flew back to the U.S. Most of us kept a calendar that showed just how many days remaining until DEROS. Each day there was drawing of a pair of boots to fill in to mark off the days. Once you got under ten days remaining you were known as a "single digit midget."

Now that I was done flying, I had to get back to Tan Son Nhut Air Base in Saigon with my few remaining personal items and go through some very detailed out processing. I packed up my remaining personal stuff that I had brought over from BMT on my fini flight day. I still had to get to Tan Son Nhut for out processing. Fortunately, there was a C-7 transport flight that landed at Quan Loi in late afternoon on December 4. That would be my freedom flight to start the process of returning home. Since we didn't return to Tan Son Nhut until late in the day, I had to wait until the next day to start my final out processing. My first stop was to the personnel office to pick up all my paperwork and begin gathering all the documents that I needed to out process.

I was met with the comment that I couldn't be out processed today because the personnel office was hastily processing those folks that were getting an early release from Vietnam. I guess my assertive FAC training kicked in and I called BS on that issue and said I would be out processed today! Right on cue the young sergeant called his boss, a master sergeant, and I had some very strong words for him. "You will start my out processing today ahead of those that haven't served in Vietnam as long as I have." I got their attention and had personal service from the master sergeant. I had to go to the equipment shop to turn in all my flying equipment, to accounting and finance to pick up my pay records, to the flight management office to pick up my Air Force Form 5 (flying records), and finally to transportation to coordinate my actual flight out of Vietnam and to find out how I could retrieve my baggage that had already been shipped to Lockbourne Air Force Base. I was able to accomplish almost all of the tasks I needed except confirming the schedule for my DEROS flight. I would have to return the next day to get that information.

That evening I decided that I would stay at the old FAC hooch that we stayed in during September and part of October. I had dinner at the Officers' Club and was kind of lost as I didn't have to get up early the next morning to fly another combat mission. Early the next morning I returned to the transportation office and got my flight information from Tan Son Nhut all the way to my home in Portland, Oregon. I would be departing the next morning, with connecting commercial flights in San Francisco and Seattle. As I looked at my flight orders, I noticed that I had a noon flight scheduled but had to report to the air terminal no later than 0700 in the morning. I questioned the transportation folks and they informed that was the correct time for check in. I spent another night in the old FAC hooch and had my last dinner in Vietnam at the Officers' Club again.

DEROS Flight: I was scheduled to fly out on a commercial, contracted DC-8 aircraft. When I arrived at the flight terminal there must have been 150 Army, Navy, Marine and Air Force troops all waiting to start the process. We were all told to take a seat as the in processing for the flight would take some time. We were also notified that we could not leave the in-processing area and the exterior doors were locked and guarded by two Army Military Police soldiers. The troops there, including me, were none too pleased with the prison-like atmosphere.

Our joy of finally leaving Vietnam was crushed by the apparent bureaucracy that was about to unfold. First, we were told to all line up and we would be administered a golden flow test, a urine test to see if any of us had drugs in our system. How humiliating. Each one of us had to fill a urine sample jar while an enlisted Army soldier observed each one of us filling the sample jar. We then had to write our name and social security number on the bottle while the soldier watched and then hand it over to the medical folks that had set up a testing lab right in the terminal area. I was not worried at all as I had never used any drugs while I was in Vietnam, but there were some very concerned faces in the crowd after they went through the golden flow process.

Next was an inspection of all our checked and carry-on baggage. I was not concerned as all I had was some flying clothes, some toiletries, and all 2,000 of the 35 mm slides that I had taken and had developed in Vietnam. I assumed that they were just looking for drugs, weapons, and any other contraband they thought was sensitive. Boy was I wrong. The Army sergeant that went through my personal stuff was a real SOB. He opened my shaving kit and then squirted all my toothpaste out of the tube and looked at every single item in the kit. He next went through each piece of clothing checking the seams, pockets, and under the collars of each shirt whether military or civilian clothing. He then went through each piece of paper of my official records one at a time looking for who knows what.

Next came the real disaster for me. Another Army sergeant came over to the inspection table and went through all 2,000 of my 35 mm slides, looking at each and every slide. He would hold each slide up to the light, look for about one second, then throw the ones he thought were sensitive into a large trash can. I protested but to no avail; he must have thrown out over half of my slides. It took him over an hour and a half to review all the slides. I had this plan to get my slides developed in Vietnam as I didn't want them to be lost in the mail having them developed in the U.S. What a huge mistake that was. It was becoming obvious why I had to show up five hours before my DEROS flight.

Once all our baggage was inspected, we were all told to go back to our seats and remain there. An Army major then addressed the crowd and said that the golden flow test was completed, and he would call out the names of those that needed further testing. He also mentioned those people whose names were called to bring their personal belongings with them. It was obvious that those twenty-five or so people would not be joining us on this flight at least. I am sure they were sent to some other holding area and stayed in Vietnam until they cleared the drug use protocol. I was good to go and couldn't wait to get on the plane.

I really don't remember the boarding process as it really didn't matter much to me. I did have a window seat, and we were once again packed in like sardines. But there were at least twenty-five open seats from those unlucky folks that didn't pass the golden flow test. Once we got airborne there was a very loud cheer from the passengers as the pilot announced our next stop would be Hickam Air Force Base in Honolulu, Hawaii for a quick refueling. I think the flight was about eleven hours, but none of us really cared much about that…we were out of Vietnam. Once again, just like the flight to Vietnam, we were not allowed to leave the boarding area of the terminal once we arrived in Hawaii. After about a two-hour delay, we all boarded the aircraft again and continued on a four-hour flight to San Francisco International Airport.

I still had two more flights to catch. All the military folks on the flight had to wear their uniforms on the flight. I was wearing my khaki brown short-sleeve uniform and had a small olive-green carry-on bag, my helmet bag. As we departed the airplane we were met by a huge number of protestors. In those days anyone could go right out to the departure and arrival gates. It was a pretty ugly scene as folks were screaming at us about being baby killers and the scum of the earth. These protesters were not all young people; there were some folks who were the same age as my parents screaming at me. How disappointing to hear that crap for doing what my country ordered me to do.

I just wanted to get to my next flight and not hear any more of the protesters. I was scheduled on an Alaska Airlines flight that would fly me into Seattle where I would catch another Alaska fight to my home in Portland. I was disappointed once again when I landed in Seattle and departed the airplane. There were more protestors at the airport but not quite as vocal as the ones in San Francisco. What had happened to our country? The next flight to Portland was uneventful and, miracles of miracles, there were no protestors inside the terminal. There were a few outside the terminal carrying very vile signs denigrating our military but by now I was numb and just ignored them. My adventure was over…I thought what an incredible experience this year in Vietnam had been. I was sure the experience had changed me in so many ways.

Chapter 10
AFTER THOUGHTS ABOUT THE WAR

So many U.S. citizens believe what they see in the movies about Vietnam veterans—that Vietnam veterans are a bunch of crazy, demented, drugged people that don't know when to stop fighting the very unpopular war. To prove this misperception by our civilian community all you have to do is look at all the protests aimed at our brave service men and women that had fought in this very unpopular war. It was not the veteran's choice to go to Vietnam but the U.S. government's decision to prosecute this war. There were no waiting crowds or bands at the airports for the returning Vietnam veterans like we see today in the U.S.

One of the most unique issues the Vietnam veteran faced was that each individual serving in Vietnam travelled and served as an individual rather than today's model when an entire unit would be deployed together. Most of the retuning veterans had been warned to expect a hostile reception when they arrived home. The animosity was pretty widespread and there were never any "Welcome Home" signs to greet our returning heroes. Many veterans hurried through the airport or even went so far as to change out of their uniform into civilian clothes at the airport to avoid the onslaught of protesters. Some veterans needed to just be invisible, to hide their trauma and try to bury their darkest experiences into silence.

My experience with the many veterans that I came across in my twenty-six-year career in the Air Force was just the opposite of that Hollywood portrayal. I guess I did not experience the trauma that many of our ground troops were exposed to. I certainly don't discount any feelings they may have developed from their combat experience. We really didn't have a name for the traumatic condition our returning Vietnam veterans had…today it is called post-traumatic stress disorder (PTSD). I did, however, believe that my experience really formed my character and how I lived following my service in Vietnam.

I have been asked many times over the years if I killed anyone in the war. I would be less than honest if I didn't agree that I probably killed a few people in the war. My role as a FAC put me at the very pointy end of the combat spear, and I certainly was involved in directing the fire power that killed many enemy troops. One of the stories I told in this book confirmed that I probably did kill a few enemy soldiers during my time in Southeast Asia. My concept was that my government had decided that this was a just war and that I had a duty to fulfill my assigned mission. I was in no position to question the legality or justification of the war while the enemy was trying to kill me just as hard as I was trying to kill him. We both had a mission to do, and I tried to do it to the best of my ability.

I was not a philosopher in the war…just a twenty-four-year-old pilot trying to stay alive. I guess I knew that I faced death on almost every flight. I had my own feelings that the war was not being conducted in the correct manner but, once again, I had a duty to fulfill and I did the best I could. So, despite the moral conflict about war, I certainly learned quite a few life lessons that served me well.

As a FAC I had a level of responsibility that I never came close to again in my future Air Force career. Never again would I have the direct power over the life and death of another person. One minor miscalculation or one moment of inattention could have meant the death of the brave ground forces I was trying to support. There was always this very same level of intensity for the decisions I made while controlling the attack and rescue aircraft that I was directing on almost every mission I flew.

Later in my career I was a flying squadron commander and did have the responsibility of sending pilots out to fly…but never in a life or death situation. We were at peace and could always cancel a flight if there was a safety issue. Not so during the war. I think the main lesson I learned was to rely on my analysis of a situation, make a judgement, and then act on that judgement and take responsibility for the outcome. I felt empowered to do the right thing in every situation, whether it was politically correct or not.

I remember the scenario when I sent a flight of F-4s off the target because their bombing accuracy was not very good. I never wavered on sending them home even though I knew I would get some feedback on the call. The call sign of the F-4 flight was Gunfighter 01 which suggested the pilot was either the squadron or wing commander. Just as I expected, I had a phone call waiting at the end of the day to call the pilot I had sent home from the bombing mission. We had a very direct discussion that I had the ultimate responsibility for the ground troops we were supporting, and I felt that his bombing ability put the ground troops in jeopardy. After some very intense feedback and grumbling he agreed with my call. I really didn't care if he agreed or not…it was the right thing to do. I guess I was getting a bit cocky with my performance, but if I always did what I thought was correct it would be a good day despite negative feedback from my peers or superiors.

Now I did have a bit of trouble with this cockiness once I returned to the States and was flying in peacetime. I was scheduled for a T-33 flight one afternoon at Eglin Air Force Base, Florida. I did the preflight briefing, preflighted my aircraft and was preparing to take off when I got a call from my operations center that I was to abort the flight due to weather. I knew the weather was above my personal minimums and asked who canceled my flight. I was told to taxi back to the squadron immediately and meet with my squadron operations officer. My operations officer, a Vietnam veteran pilot, forcefully reminded me that I was no longer in Vietnam, that the rules for flying were different in the States, and if I wanted to succeed in the Air Force I needed to start paying attention to his guidance. The light came on and I knew that I was now operating under a different set of rules. Deep down I knew he was right, but I always tried throughout my career to do what I thought was correct and then take responsibility for my actions.

While I still have my doubts about the overall war effort in Vietnam, I feel that I did the duty that my country asked me to do. If I could have been king for a day as the Commander-in-Chief I would have let our military do its job: attack the enemy where it would hurt the most, and eliminate all the safe and no fire zones, bombing restrictions, and the ubiquitous rules of engagement. I would have destroyed the enemy's war supplies before they got dispersed into the county side. I would have destroyed the North Vietnam fighter aircraft on the ground and destroyed the SAM sites before they were operational.

The U.S. strategy was to contain the spread of global communism. This, I believe, was a noble cause because in the sixties country after country fell to the false promise of communism. Our political leaders at the time thought communism was a serious threat to our national security. I was certainly in no position to doubt the motives of our government…I was there to do my duty. But I was just a small cog in the overall effort of the United States. I was proud of the way I grew as a person and military leader.

The skills and lessons I learned during my time at war were a huge factor in developing my character in the years that followed Vietnam. I would not trade my war experience for anything. The Vietnam experience made me the person I am today…good or bad, this is who I am. I learned to do the right thing even if it is not politically correct at the time. I also learned to do it now…

don't procrastinate with your decisions. If you get better information after the decision, change the decision but never ever wait for perfect information with which to make a decision. I hope this summary of my memories as a FAC can answer the question that will probably come from one or more of my six grandchildren, "Grampa what did you do in the war?"

Chapter 11
HONORING MY FALLEN BROTHERS IN ARMS

As I continued my Air Force career and my follow-on retirement consulting career, I thought back on all of the sacrifices that my fellow FACs and support staff had given to our country. Almost by accident I found out that there was a local group of former Vietnam FACs in Colorado Springs that got together for breakfast once a month. Even though it had been thirty-six years since I was in Vietnam, I immediately bonded with these former FACs. Our war stories were better each time we heard them or told them. It was good to be talking about our experiences. It was also heartening to see the other FACs who were also aging "gracefully," just like me.

In early 2007 the local Colorado Springs FACs decided to host the FAC reunion that was held every two years and planned for October 2008. As I was sitting at breakfast, in a moment of weakness, I agreed to be on the FAC Memorial Committee. Our goal was to build a granite memorial for the nearly 300 "slow" FACs and support staff that had been killed in the war in Southeast Asia. The Misty "fast" F-100 FACs also joined us and added a separate granite monument to honor the eight Misty FACs killed in Southeast Asia. It turned out to be a huge project. We had to come up with a design, hire a company to build the monument, secure $75,000 in contributions, determine what names should be on the memorial, and finally develop and schedule the dedication ceremony. It became an almost full-time job, but what a pleasure working with other FACs again.

Our FAC memorial team validated each name that we would engrave on our memorial. We used an existing FAC Association listing of those FACs killed in action. We cross-referenced each name with the Vietnam Veterans Memorial Virtual Wall web site to confirm we had everyone listed. We also wanted to ensure that we didn't add any names that were not legitimate FAC-associated personnel. We included members of all U.S. services and a couple of Vietnamese officers that were also killed performing the FAC mission. During preparation for the FAC memorial, while I was trying to track down any surviving members of the FACs that we were honoring, I decided to check the virtual Vietnam Veterans Memorial web page. Our plan was to find as many surviving family members and invite them to the memorial dedication ceremony. While on the Vietnam Veterans Memorial Virtual Wall web page I found a very moving tribute that had been written to James Newendorp, the pilot whose body I had flown to the morgue in October 1971, by his surviving son, Eric. Here is the tribute that I found:

> Thank you for your love and sacrifice and sense of duty and honor for this great nation. Nobody can ever know how deep it runs, or how important it is. And we all—every citizen of this country—should never, ever forget what you and hundreds of thousands of others like you, throughout the course of the history of this still young nation, did for us and have given to us. There is NO GREATER SACRIFICE. Your influence is felt by me and is part of me every day. I am sorry we never knew each other like a father and son should, but although it makes my heart heavy, and as hard as it may be sometimes, I understand. Amazing how you can have this level of respect for someone you never knew. I feel for you. Eric, Friday, June 17, 2005.

I searched Eric Newendorp's name on Google and found a listing at Tulsa University in the athletic department. I immediately called and talked to him about my experience of flying his father's body on his last mission in Vietnam. He was more than happy to hear from me as he had very little information about the mission that his father was killed on. He wanted to hear as much information as I had on the fateful day that he lost his father. Over the following months we talked quite often, and Eric coordinated with me to meet the rest of his family members during a reunion in Golden, Colorado during the weekend of July 4, 2008. What a moving event, and I was able to give the family some additional closure on the death of their loved one.

The 2008 FAC Memorial dedication ceremony was spectacular. We had nearly 1,500 people show up for the dedication ceremony. It was held at Colorado Springs Memorial Park, and we were honored to have retired Colonel Bud Day, a former Misty FAC who was awarded the Medal of Honor for his bravery and professionalism during his POW captivity in Hanoi for nearly six years, as our dedication speaker. Just as awesome was the fact that we had tracked down nearly fifty family members of our fallen FACs. We prepared seats of honor for them in the front row of the dedication ceremony. With the very generous amount of donations we were able to pay a large part of the honored families' travel expenses. In some cases, this was the very first time these honored families had been involved in a ceremony recognizing the sacrifice their father, husband, or brother made to our country.

In addition to the very moving twenty-one-gun salute, we coordinated a flyover by an 0-1, an 0-2, and four F-16 fighters from the Colorado National Guard. One other superb part of the dedication ceremony was the support of the Patriot Guard Riders (PGR). The PGRs are a nationwide group of U.S. veterans that provide motorcycle escorts to protect family members of fallen veterans. The bikers escorted the busses carrying the family members from the hotel to the memorial site, and then about twenty-five members of the PGR stood in formation holding U.S. flags surrounding the memorial site.

It was a magical time connecting with many of the folks I had flown with so many years ago. As I was requesting funds for the memorial, I was asked by a potential donor why we were building the FAC Memorial. This kind of set me back and I had to think about that question. But after more thought I determined this was a valid question…why the FAC Memorial? I decided the best way to answer this question, as I bet other folks had the same question, would be to write an editorial in the local newspaper describing why we were building the FAC Memorial. The words of the editorial certainly, in my mind at least, answered the Why the FAC Memorial question. The guest editorial was placed in the Colorado Springs daily newspaper, The Gazette, on the day of the FAC Memorial dedication ceremony, October 3, 2008. That editorial is reprinted below:

> As I was discussing the Forward Air Controller (FAC) Memorial with a potential donor, he asked me why are you building a memorial to the FACs? Didn't those pilots die a long time ago? At first, I really didn't have an answer other than a friend of mine in the FAC Association asked if I would be on the committee to help build the memorial.
>
> But the more I thought about his question the more I really understood why I was involved in this project. The real story of my involvement in the FAC Memorial started over 37 years ago as I was completing my one-year tour in South East Asia as a 0-2A Forward Air Controller. The FAC mission was one of the most dangerous flying missions in Southeast Asia and FAC pilots accounted for three Medals of Honor, 25 Air Force Crosses, numerous Silver Stars, hundreds of Distinguished Flying crosses and thousands of Air Medals. Almost 300 FACs and support staff members were killed flying and supporting this very dangerous mission.

Fortunately, I was a very young pilot, my first assignment following pilot training, so it was no big deal to me. I guess the old saying "ignorance is bliss" applied to me and I wanted to fly as many hours as I could to build up my flying time.

I was a young and impressionable Air Force Lt. and knew that the Viet Nam war was not too popular on the home front. I really didn't pay much attention to what was going on back home. That was until I heard another young veteran, who would later run for and win a seat in the U.S. Senate in Massachusetts tell us on Armed Forces TV that all the veterans in Vietnam were a bunch of killers and behaved much like Genghis Kahn. There I was in April 1971 in the pilot's hooch in Bien Hoa with my fellow pilots watching this supposed war hero disrespecting all the veterans that had fought or were still fighting in the Viet Nam war. I was very offended by his remarks and knew that what he was saying was absolutely false. I never saw a single incident take place that he mentioned. But I was a pilot and flew above that kind of activity. Not true. I was a FAC assigned to the 5th Special Forces Group and was stationed in the field with these brave soldiers and ate, drank and conducted missions with them on a daily basis. They were true professionals in every sense of the word. But the "horror" stories of Viet Nam seemed to be the big story of the day in our then, only mainstream media.

Finally, after 535 combat sorties or 237 combat missions (when I was a FAC the Air Force counted a FAC combat mission as the number of sorties flown in a 24-hour day) and 752 hours of combat flying my tour came to an end and I returned to the states. Not really surprising to me I had a very unfriendly homecoming when I returned. The protesters greeted me at the San Francisco airport and were shouting the standard hate speech at the time about us being a bunch of baby killers and much worse. The protesters also greeted me in the Seattle airport when I transferred planes for my flight to my home in Portland Oregon. It was a very bad time in our country. The nation was as badly divided as it is today with the Iraq war and the only thing we heard then, as now, was the bad news from the war. My fellow brothers in arms were dying in a very unpopular war or coming home terribly wounded, physically, mentally and spiritually. I felt betrayed by the American people. I had seen some of my best friends make the ultimate sacrifice for their country. I felt that their sacrifice, their dedication, their patriotism and their beliefs had become irrelevant and they were loathed by much of our country including a future president, U.S. Senators and other leaders of our country. I decided right then and there that I would do something to honor those brave men that made the ultimate sacrifice. Little did I know that it would be another 37 years to make good on that promise.

The delay in my actions was due in large part to me continuing my career in the Air Force and obviously not being able to speak out about the terrible treatment our veterans were enduring from the liberal political left wing in our country. After the Air Force, my consulting career got in the way and I was just too busy to do what I knew needed to be done. But as my consulting career slowed down I realized that I was seeing some of the very same things in our country that I had seen during the Viet Nam war…the betrayal and disrespect of our troops from the liberals that were so vile to us during the Viet Nam war. I was hearing almost the same rhetoric from the same people including the very same U.S. senator from Massachusetts, and other top-level leaders for that party. Just as the left in America worshiped the so called "war hero" veteran in 1971 this same bunch of people were now making a hero out of a make-believe soldier that related the terrible atrocities that he had seen taking place in the Iraq war. Sounded very familiar to the phony stories I heard that day in 1971 from a future U.S. Senator. Only problem with these tales of the current day "hero" was the stories were also not true. The main stream media was also at it again distorting the story of the current Iraq war and the scenario was there all over again…a nasty disrespect of our military veterans from one of the two major political parties in our country and our immoral main stream media. While I could do very little except complain about the current state of disrespect of our soldiers, sailors and airmen from most of the liberals in our country at least I could try to honor the brave men that died in a previous unpopular war.

The time was right to correct that injustice to our brave men and women from so long ago. So that is why I am involved in this memorial project…to bring some long-forgotten honor to the brave men that I flew with so many years ago, those men that gave the ultimate sacrifice to their country and to give them a place of honor that they were deprived of for so long.

Our FAC Memorial will be a very stunning granite monument listing the names of the 297 pilots and support staff, both officer and enlisted, that were killed flying the FAC mission from all-over South-East Asia. We have chosen Memorial Park in Colorado Springs as the site for the monument. The FAC Memorial will be located within the military section of the park, very near the Purple Heart Memorial. The Memorial will have Pikes Peak as the prominent background. The names of the three FAC Medal of Honor recipients, (one still living) will also be predominantly displayed on the memorial. This living Medal of Honor recipient, Colonel Bud Day, is our invited dedication speaker.

As part of our dedication ceremony we will also hand out, with the dedication program, a detailed history of the FAC mission from the very early days of WWII right up until today in the war in Southwest Asia. We must never forget the mission that these brave men flew and died doing for our country. Check out our Memorial web page at: http://www.fac-assoc.org/2008facmemorialPage2.htm

Part of the design of the Memorial will have four engraved sandstone inscriptions on the concrete base of the monument that captures the very essence of what we are trying to do.

"It is foolish and wrong to mourn the men who died. Rather we should thank God that such men lived." General George S. Patton

"Greater love has no man than this, that a man gave his life for his friends." John 15:13

Forward Air Controllers: Men who flew willingly to the sound of battle.

If not for the FAC many more names would be inscribed on the Vietnam Veterans' Memorial Wall.

I did get some very positive feedback from my fellow FACs about the editorial. It captured many of the same thoughts they had about their time in Vietnam. This 2008 FAC Memorial was not the last time I was involved in honoring our fallen FAC brothers. The Colorado Springs FAC Association was blessed by the fact that there was a squadron of "new" FACs stationed at Fort Carson a few miles south of downtown Colorado Springs.

The new FACs are now called Joint Terminal Attack Controllers or JTACs. Because of the vast improvement of ground-to-air guns and missiles the small, light aircraft that we flew in Southeast Asia would be much too vulnerable for today's wartime environment. The new FACs today do what the FACs did in

Southeast Asia, only they do it exclusively from the ground. With the advent of GPS and laser guided munitions they have become very effective doing the FAC mission in Afghanistan, Iraq, and other places in Southwest Asia and around the world. The new FAC squadron is called the 13th Air Support Operations Squadron or ASOS. When we found out that this new Air Force squadron was in the "neighborhood" we invited ourselves down to their squadron to get to know the new FACs and share the legacy of the FAC mission with them.

We became very close to the squadron and many times six to ten members of the squadron joined the old FACs at our monthly breakfast. The entire squadron would then show up as we cleaned and tidied up the FAC memorial each May for Memorial Day celebrations. One year, the squadron's operations officer, Major Walter D. Gray, led the squadron clean-up team with the old FACs. It was very heartwarming sharing FAC stories with each other. Then disaster stuck. We got word that Major Gray had been killed in action in Afghanistan the following August. We were all stunned. The old FACs wanted to do something to recognize the sacrifice of the new FACs, as over the years six JTACs had been killed in action.

We decided that we would put the old 2008 FAC Memorial Planning Team back in place and add a granite monument for the new FACs and place it on the same pad where we had the names of the nearly 300 FACs that were killed in Southeast Asia. The design was very straight forward, and our pad for the granite was already in place. We again began soliciting donations for the new memorial. We wanted to keep the same concept as the 2008 memorial and invite as many of the fallen heroes' family members as we could find. The task was much easier this time around as all of the JTACs killed in action had been lost within the last five years. Through some fine detective work were able to find family members for all six fallen heroes. The donations exceeded our expectations, and we were able to pay for the travel expenses of the thirty-five family members that attended the memorial dedication in 2013. On an even brighter note we found that during the 2008 FAC memorial we had left a name of a fallen FAC, Lieutenant Colonel Andrew Matyas, off the memorial. We did not find the name of this fallen FAC until about 2011. We had to rectify that.

Once again, we did some very fine detective work and found two daughters and a grandson of Lieutenant Colonel Matyas living in Maine. Neither one of the daughters knew much about their father's death as they were very young children when he died in 1968. We immediately invited them to the JTAC memorial service, paid for their travel expenses and added their father's name to the 2008 FAC memorial granite slab.

Major John Duffy, a highly decorated Special Forces soldier, really summed up the essence of the Forward Air Controller in his famous Requiem to the Forward Air Controller that he wrote for the 2008 Memorial Dedication ceremony:

"It is the lonely mission, The Forward Air Controller.
His are the eyes above the battle. He is the link to those below.
While others avoid and strike fast, He lingers and trolls for contact,
seeking out the enemy below, determining the strike force needed.
His is the job to control the air attack; He determines the needs of the troops and works the airstrike margins. His judgment is relied upon by all. Watching a "FAC" roll in hot on target, all guns blazing at his destruction, is to watch a man of courage in action. This is the daily job of the "FAC".

Major John J. Duffy, DSC, U.S. Army Retired

About the Publisher, Tactical 16

The victor always writes the history, but oftentimes that history is written by someone that neither served nor lived during the conflict. Tactical 16 is on a mission to write the history of America's conflicts by those who experienced them—all of it, the messy and chaotic, and the tragic, the stories of good people in dangerous situations and the wrong people that made conditions perilous, as well as the politics and policies that impacted organizations at a fundamental level for better or worse.

Aside from helping to preserve history and assisting those with PTSD during the writing process, Tactical 16 has published books in children's, business, leadership, and fiction genres. They continue to look for those unique stories that are uncommonly told by civilians, veterans and first responders young and old.

The name Tactical 16 has two parts. Tactical refers to the armed forces, police, fire and rescue communities. The "16" is the number of acres destroyed on September 11, 2001, at Ground Zero.

My hope is that the proceeds of this book will help the men and women who served this country when she called. I encourage other members of my community to tell their story.

www.ingramcontent.com/pod-product-compliance
Lightning Source LLC
Chambersburg PA
CBHW041317110526
44591CB00021B/2821